GAME
OF EXTREMES
25 EXCEPTIONAL
SOCCER
STORIES

ROY LINGSTER

A GAME OF EXTREMES: 25 EXCEPTIONAL SOCCER STORIES

WHAT HAPPENS ON AND OFF THE FIELD

ROY LINGSTER

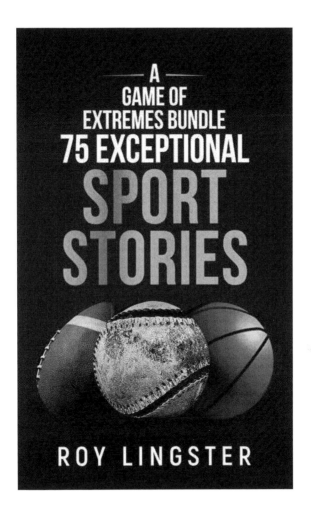

No matter how big of a sports fan you are, there is always something more to know about the games and the players.

What is it about these sports legends that amazes their fans and leaves them awestruck?

Do you want to look behind the scenes of the most consequential moments in football, basketball, and baseball?

If you answered yes, then you are in the perfect place to discover a heavy dose of inspiration and enlightenment!

As you read through these pages, you'll unravel **75 of the most captivating anecdotes** of sports who showcased exemplary courage and defied all odds, serving as a beacon of hope for ordinary people.

This unique bundle is packed with the stories of triumph, defeat, and challenges of some of the most incredible athletes who **inspired millions, set new records, and led their sports to new heights.**

Inside these pages, you will discover:

- A riveting account of the baseball rockstar, *Zack Greinke*—and his unusual rider requests that kept him in the spotlight
- The incredible story of a baseball phenom, *Sidd Finch*—and how he became **one of the biggest hoaxes in sports history**

- A journey through the inspiring life of a local sports coach—and his role in inventing the game of basketball
- From battling racism to inspiring renaissance—take an exciting dive into the stories of **one of the best basketball teams you've probably never heard of**
- **Highlights from the enticing life of** *Allen Iverson*—the prison punk who went on to become one of the most celebrated NBA stars
- A closer look into football's epic blowout defeats, including when the Chicago Bears beat Washington by 73–0
- **Electrifying snippets from the 2012 football game that was won in just 52 seconds**

And so much more!

You'll learn more than just the surface-level facts and really understand what goes into the making of truly memorable sports lore.

CONTENTS

INTRODUCTION

"To see the ball, to run after it, makes me the happiest man in the world."

— DIEGO MARADONA

For more than 100 years and despite many changes throughout the world, one thing has remained remarkably consistent: no matter what part of Earth you are on, soccer is incredibly popular.

There are a few exceptions to this rule, of course, but the fact remains that few sports have the global reach that soccer does. From young children in backyards to professional sports players making millions a year, soccer has touched the lives of so many.

And its popularity actually only increases as the years go on. Even countries like the United States, which has long been a holdout when it comes to loving soccer, is becoming more accustomed to and intrigued by the sport. That is why World Cup viewership in the United States is at an all-time high.

There is just something about soccer that fires up the people who play it and the people who watch it. There is truly no other sport in the world that gets people so engaged, so driven, so passionate, and so devoted. You see it again and again in the faces of fans who chant and sing and scream and cry with every play of the game. You also see it in the anguished looks of defeat or fevered looks of excitement on players and coaches during defeats and victories.

Soccer has been around for a long time but it was created as a deviation from another popular sport: rugby. Rugby, a sport that still looks a lot like soccer, was incredibly prominent in many parts of the world. In the 1800s, it was one of the most popular sports around.

But it was becoming increasingly complicated and as the sport grew and spread, it was confusing people.

There were certain rugby teams who played predominantly with their hands while others used their feet more. As you can imagine, this made playing confounding when two teams from different regions met up for a match.

From that, soccer was born. The teams that played more with the feet started to evolve and change the game. Over time, it officially became its own sport. Soccer—or football as it is known throughout most of the world—instantly became a hit with many people, rugby fans who were looking for something faster, a bit more fun, less violent, but just as challenging.

In 1863, a group of schools met to create a set of rules to manage soccer and push it to the next level. From there, competitions and leagues were formed. The Football Association further focused on the lack of hands in the game, giving soccer its most well-known feature and trickiest rule.

Within just a few years, more and more people were adopting this new game, and it became a hit seemingly overnight.

It's not hard to see why soccer was a smash from the very beginning. Players do not need much to get started. Learning the rules of the game only takes a few moments, not much equipment is needed, you can play it anywhere. It became the sort of sport that almost anyone—rich or poor, experienced or novice—could get into. It was soon a universal language that was spoken in every part of the world.

The quote above, from Diego Maradona, perfectly summarizes what makes soccer so special and why it's had such an impact on so many people for more than 100 years now. For many people, soccer is more than a sport. It is more than just scoring points and dancing on the field and celebrating with teammates.

No, for many people, soccer is something that can literally change lives, bring nations together, and speak to a deep-seated and very authentic emotion that few people get to experience. The joy that is felt during victory is unlike any other. The commitment felt by both fans and players is unparalleled. In so many ways, soccer is way more than simply a sport. It is filled with inspiring moments, heroic champions, and an enthusiasm that remains unmatched.

The truth is that for more than 100 years, there have been many stories, rich in history, about soccer. The good, the bad, and the ugly have been witnessed on the soccer field. And true soccer fans don't want a sterilized version of the game and its rich history. No, they want to know it all. Every up and down, every peak and valley, every good and bad moment. They want it all.

That is what you will get in this book. It doesn't matter if you are new to soccer or if you have enjoyed it all your life; within these pages, you will get a crash course in so many of the best stories that summarize the importance and power of this game that is loved by billions.

For years now, I have been studying the game, compiling the greatest factoids, and becoming an expert on all things soccer. I have selected only the very best of the best when it comes to stories and historical figures who have played the game. We are not going to jump into the most well-known tales revolving around soccer. Instead, we are going to dig into the things that most people don't know.

When you have turned the last page of this book, you will know so much more about soccer and the impact it's had on the people who play it, the people who love it, and the world at large. Because it is true that soccer has quite literally changed the world. It's not often that a sport can bring entire nations and communities closer together, but that's exactly what soccer has done. There is a reason for that, and you will learn all the ways that soccer can affect the world.

Unlike some sports, soccer hasn't been around for hundreds of years. It is a relatively new sport in many ways. Yet the ways that it has grown and flourished during its life are immense and impressive. All of this was accomplished because of the hard-working, incredible people who made the game what it is today.

To learn about soccer is to learn about the world and all sorts of people in different walks of life, from every corner of the globe. Studying this game isn't studying a sport, it's studying a lifestyle.

If you are ready to learn much more about soccer, then you have come to the right place. There are literally hundreds upon hundreds of compelling stories about this game, but in the pages ahead, you will learn of the 25 that best summarize this sport that has shaped generations.

1

THE GAME THAT LED TO A
100-HOUR WAR

As mentioned in the introduction, a lot of great things have come from the game of soccer. Families, friends, and entire nations have come together because of the game and it has a great unifying effect on the people who participate in and love it.

But it cannot be denied that soccer can also have a negative impact on people. This is true for any sport, but soccer has often ignited the strongest emotions in people, sometimes negative.

In fact, it has actually led to a legitimate war.

The quote that opened this book spoke about how soccer is so much more than just a game and is more of a feeling of elation, freedom, and humanity. But another quote should be remembered when speaking of soccer, that from Eduard Galeano, who said,"The Soccer War is thus a bloody reminder that the implications of sport can reach far beyond the field."

What is the Soccer War, how did it begin, and why is this great sport to blame for bloodshed?

We need to venture back to the early twentieth century and Central America, where tensions had never been higher. The entire continent had been suffering and often battling during that period, mostly due to the rise of poor economic conditions for millions of people.

El Salvador was just one of the nations that was suffering due to economic hardships. At that point in the country's history, El Salvador was mostly owned by rich people and there was little farmland for anyone who wasn't making as much money as them. There was constant fighting for the land that was available, so the impoverished farmers could stake their claim and make some money for themselves and their families.

Nearby Honduras was experiencing a similar problem. There were millions of farmers attempting to win their own land and take it back from the rich people who held it so tightly.[1] The only difference between the two countries was that Honduras had more than five times as much space as El Salvador did.[2]

Because of this, there were millions of Salvadorans who left their homes in hopes of finding something better in Honduras. This led to a rise in tensions between the two countries, as the people in Honduras weren't happy about seeing so many people come into their country.

By 1969, more than 300,000 Salvadorans had come to live in Honduras, making up 20 percent of the peasant population of that nation.

In that same year, the soccer teams from the two countries were fighting it out in the World Cup. At that point, there had already been some violence between fans in previous games but tensions had never been higher, mostly because of the economic and political conditions between the countries at the time.

During the second qualifying round for the 1969 FIFA World Cup, Honduras and El Salvador faced off. On June 8, 1969, in the Honduran city of Tegucigalpa, there was violence among spectators during the opening match, which Honduras won 1–0.[3]

Even more bloodshed ensued after El Salvador's 3–0 victory in the second game, played on June 15 in San Salvador, the capital of El Salvador.

On June 26, 1969, a playoff game was held in Mexico City.[4] After extra time, El Salvador prevailed in the third and final game, 3–2. The Honduran government,

El Salvador claimed, "Has not taken any effective measures to punish these crimes that constitute genocide, nor has it given assurances of indemnification or reparations for the damages caused to Salvadorans." As a result, El Salvador severed its diplomatic relationship with Honduras.

That was only the start of the conflict that exploded in the days ahead. On July 14, 1969, the war officially began. Attacks inside Honduras were intense and violent right away and within four days, 3,000 people would lose their lives and hundreds of thousands lost their homes.

The war didn't last long and a ceasefire was called on July 18 and took effect on July 20, with El Salvador finally withdrawing from Honduras on August 2, 1969. All of the damage and the lives lost were caused because of reasons beyond soccer, but there is no doubt that the World Cup games definitely had an impact on the two nations and brought them to the brink of war.

While soccer can be seen as a force for greatness in the world, it can also lead to a lot of conflict and angry feelings, not only between people but entire countries. While tensions have flared between parties during soccer games, nothing comes close to the 100-Hour War, often called the Football War because of the spark that started the flames of war.

Thankfully, since then, there hasn't been anything like the Football War. While there is still an occasional fight at soccer games, no match has led to armed conflict between two distinct countries since this dark moment in soccer's history.

2

FRESH WOUNDS OF A DIFFERENT KIND

"If I could apologize and go back and change history I would do. But the goal is still a goal, Argentina became world champions and I was the best player in the world."

— DIEGO MARADONA

What is one of the few things that everyone, no matter how much they have played, knows about soccer?

It's probably the fact that the game is played with just feet and head, no hands. In fact, not using your hands in soccer is perhaps the most prominent and well-known rule that every soccer pro takes to heart.

However, there was one instance where the use of a hand not only decided a game but an entire championship. And it wasn't just any championship either, it was a deciding game that had a lot to do with not just soccer but the world at large and international conflict.

The year was 1986 and Argentina was facing off against the English soccer team. All the pressure was on star player Diego Maradona, who was thought to be Argentina's best chance at claiming victory and bringing the trophy home to his country.[1]

There was a lot more on the line than simply that victory. That is because Argentina and the United Kingdom had been at war only a few years before. The Falklands War was an armed conflict during the summer of 1982, and the wounds from that war were still fresh in the hearts and minds of Argentinian people.[2] They were watching the game not only because they were rooting for their team but because they were rooting for their country, too.

It had been some time since these two squads battled it out on the field and there were many people who felt that the UK was using unfair advantages to give them an upper hand. Numerous Argentinians felt that this

England-based match was discriminating against them. Language issues were a huge, pressing problem for their squad. For instance, when referees tried to eject Argentina's captain from the game, he didn't understand their English. Officials did little to help the visiting Argentina team better understand the language and much context was lost in translation.

This illustrates how exclusion remained in the soccer community and how particular teams that didn't speak English were considered "less than" and not as important or capable as others.

So not only was there anger about the language barrier that was holding Argentina back, but more importantly, the festering, unavoidable resentment of England because of its involvement in Argentina was downright palpable and felt throughout the game. Numerous commentators and analysts noted that the game served as a channel for Argentina's general indignation of England's abuse of power, particularly during the Falklands War.

Fifty minutes into the much-watched match, no team had scored a goal, leaving the score 0–0. Then, in minute 51, Diego Maradona made good on his promise of scoring a goal for his team. He used his head to knock the ball into the goal, giving the game its first point.

However, if you look back at the footage today, you will see that Maradona actually didn't use only his head to hit the ball into the goal. In fact, his raised first, not his head, was the one that did the trick. That is why the goal is today referred to as the "Hand of God" goal.

Back in the 1980s, referees didn't have the ability to rewatch footage of the game and see if they made the right call or not. Therefore, the goal stood as called and everyone thought that Argentina was ahead rightfully. British player Gary Lineker, who would score the only goal for England, actually called it the best goal he had ever seen.

Argentina would win that year's World Cup, which was a huge moment for the team and the country that was still reeling from the war from just a few years before. Over the years, there have been conflicting opinions about the game and the "Hand of God" goal, but one thing is obvious: this goal not only lifted the spirits of the players but also the country watching at home.

A monument to the long-lasting effects of imperial interference in Argentina and the surrounding area, this contentious triumph from 1986 continues to be a huge source of pride for the nation and for Latin America as a whole. This instance also exemplifies how common perseverance and strength help to develop collective, cultural memories, such as those of the 1986 World Cup for Latin America.

It is yet another example of the power of the game of soccer. Whether the goal was unjust or not, it was able to speak to people who were looking for positive news that could help them feel closer together and move beyond war. The players on the field weren't treated fairly, and they knew they had the cards stacked against them. But they never gave up, they never stopped fighting for their country, and they did whatever was necessary to secure a victory.

Years later, it is clear that this pivotal goal was a major moment in soccer history. It might not have been called the correct way at the time, but the impact it had then and now is still monumental.

3

HOW MANY PENALTIES?

"Penalties are only missed by those who have the courage to take them."

— ROBERTO BAGGIO

You may have only a passing knowledge of penalty kicks in soccer if you haven't played the game much. No one would blame you for not understanding the particulars of the game, including penalty kicks, or PKs, unless you've played or watched a good deal of soccer.

In the game, a match can be decided by penalty kicks. If a game ends in a draw, each team will step and take a shot at the goal that is unrestricted, aside from the goalie who is the only hope of victory.[1]

Usually, a sudden death like this is determined by a couple of goals, sometimes only one. But let's take a look at the long shoot-out in soccer history. It wasn't just sort of long, it was jaw-droppingly, unbelievably, shockingly long and lives on to this day.

Fourth Division Argentinian soccer doesn't get a whole lot of attention, but those who like it love it an awful lot. And they got their money's worth during one game in the 2009/10 season. In the Apertura's qualifying round for the Ronda Final at the end of the season, a game featuring Juventud Alianza[2] versus General Paz Juniors[3] was set to determine which team advanced and which team's season was over. Undoubtedly, this game had a lot on the line.

The game ended in a 3–3 tie, which obviously wouldn't do. That meant that a round of penalty kicks was on the agenda. But you'll never believe just how long they were kicking for.

What happened next was a 21–20 shootout that seemed like it would never end. That means that each of those attempted goals—until the very last one—found the goal and scored a point. Back and forth the two teams went, each taking a shot and sinking it, furthering the game and mountain even more tension. The only missed goal was the last one, which was missed by Juventud Alianza goalkeeper Gonzalez. He missed every shot before that too, of course, but it was that last one that counted the most.

Imagine being in the crowd on that day. Imagine being a diehard fan of one of those teams and the feelings of anxiety and tension each and every time the player stepped up and sent the ball flying to the goal. Now imagine the joy you would have felt when the ball actually connected with the goal and another penalty kick was counted. You would think that your team was surely going to win now, right?

Now, imagine sitting there for kick after kick, goal after goal, score after score, with no end in sight. The thrill would surely wear off and, soon, you'd be feeling something akin to agitation and worry. There were probably a countless number of fans who were chewing their nails off during this wild, hard-to-believe knockout.

But while that was an intense shootout that seemed like it would never end, it wasn't the only one in the history of soccer. In 2005, KK Palace and the Civics were duking it out in the Namibian Cup. The game concluded with a tied 2–2 score. Following that, there were 48 penalty kicks with some players having to step up to kick the ball three times.

The shootout was seemingly endless until it ended with a 17–16 PK score for KK Palace. Both sides of the field were completely exhausted from the shootout, as were the fans who still hadn't lost their voices after hours of crying out and cheering on their squad.

But if you want to talk about the longest soccer shootout in the history of the world, you will have to return to 2022. Two non-league teams from England were in a match called the Memorial Cup. The teams of Washington and Bedlington tied their match at 3–3 before they went toe-to-toe and shot a combined 49 penalty kicks. In the end, Washington took the top prize with a 25–24 penalty kick score.

The amount of time it takes for a penalty kick to be lined up and pulled off is a couple of minutes. That means that fans were standing in the arena for far more than an hour, with each and every attempt stealing all of their attention and focus. Each kick was a triumph, but then each one was met with sadness when the other team followed it up with a goal of their own. It's tiring just to think about it.

The fact that penalty kicks are so important is a pretty telling fact. That is because soccer, at its core, is really all about kicking the ball, of course. Therefore, it makes sense that these high-tension and important games ended with a series of crucial kicks.

These games are examples that soccer can be one of the most intense games in the world, even though it's basically just a simple premise: kick a ball into a goal. These intense, lengthy shootouts show that there are few things as exhilarating, disappointing, and unique as a penalty kick shootout in soccer.

Soccer will always be a game about sinking a ball into a goal. And these games show that no matter all the tricks and skills and jaw-dropping abilities that players learn, there is nothing more important than simply being able to connect the ball with the netting in the goal. These games will go down in history, even though they didn't feature the biggest names in the game, because they stand as a testament to just how wild and special the game of soccer can be.

4

THE GREATEST SOCCER COMEBACK

"It's hard to beat somebody who never gives up."

— MEGAN RAPINOE

What is something that you know about all sports, and in fact, all challenges in life?

It's probably the fact that, no matter what and no matter what is stacked against you, you should never, ever give up on something you really want. You have likely been told this before at many points in your life. You have school teachers, friends, family members, and bosses who have said that you *can* achieve anything, even when success seems out of reach.

Indeed, the only thing stopping you from accomplishing whatever you want is yourself. You can get in your own way and a lack of belief is a surefire way to lose any chance of winning.

This is especially true in sports. And it's even more true when it comes to soccer. In soccer, a goal can literally make or break a game because so many matches are low-scoring. Therefore, in just the span of a few minutes, the entire fate of a team can change from one direction to the complete opposite.

Back in 1957, that is a lesson that the Charlton Athletic soccer team learned very well.

Huddersfield Town was going through a normal season that year under the new leadership of Bill Shankly, who was attempting to find new levels of success for the team he was now managing. Little did he know that his team would be a part of one of the biggest comebacks in soccer history.

If only his team would be on the right side of that historic game.

Aside from Shankly's hiring, a lot of big changes were coming for Town at the time. Vic Metcalfe made his final appearance in their jersey during the season in a game versus Sheffield United in March. This was a massive sea change for the team and it meant that every victory was going to mean a whole lot more—but so was every defeat.

Then there was the game at The Valley on December 21, 1957, a contest with Charlton Athletic. The two teams had met three times before and had given fans a few very intense, fun, high-scoring games. But they had no idea that they were about to embark on something that had never been seen before, or after.

To put it bluntly, Town was absolutely decimating Charlton. Town was well on their way to beating Charlton and gaining another success. After just 27 minutes left in the game, the score was 5–1 in Town's favor. In a game of soccer, teams sometimes don't score for 10 to 15 minutes at a time. There was legitimately very little chance of Charlton being able to come back from such a deficit.

Fans of the team had pretty much resigned themselves to that fact and were ready to just let the match end and prepare for the next one.

But then something miraculous happened.

Town held a 5–1 lead with 27 minutes to go[1] and Charlton played with just 10 men for the remainder of the game. But then, one after another, the squad playing for Charlton started scoring goal after goal.

It was hard to slow, stop, and overcome the onslaught brought by the Charlton. With less than a half hour before the game was over, Charlton did something seemingly impossible. Not only did they catch up with Town, they actually overtook them in the score box.

When the game was over, the fans and both teams were left stunned. Charlton ended up winning the match, 7–6, over Town. Not only did Town think they were going to win the game, but they thought they were going to win it easily. The fact that they lost was shocking, especially when they were so far ahead of Charlton for most of the game.

There has only been one game in professional soccer history when a team scored six goals and still lost. Amazingly, 24 goals were scored in the four games that Town and Charlton played against each other that season.[2] During that year, a rivalry was born and it was one that would last for years. Town would win many more games, as would Charlton over the years. But no one would ever forget that one game in the 1957–58 season when the impossible was made possible.

Some people will complain about soccer because it's typically a low-scoring game. It is not often that a team scores more than a few points. In fact, many games are won by just one point, and there are plenty that end in a draw with no one scoring a single goal.

But the fact that soccer is low-scoring doesn't mean it's boring. Quite the opposite is true, in fact. Soccer is all about strategy and might and drive. It's all about playing your heart out for the entirety of the game. The match between Town and Charlton shows that. Yes, the game was a high scoring one in relation to other soccer games but it wasn't about the 7–6 score. That's not what made it exciting. What really makes this game one for the record book is that one team never counted itself out, even when it was down in a bad way and victory seemed downright impossible.

Charlton didn't stop fighting, they didn't stop believing in themselves. And, in the end, that made the difference and allowed them to win the game. Games like these are a great reminder of just how important perseverance is in all sports, but most especially soccer. The game is only over when one team no longer believes that it can win. When they feel defeated, they will probably *be* defeated.

5

WHEN ONE'S OWN GOAL ISN'T ENOUGH

W e have all had moments in our lives when we are feeling the pressure.

Whether it be an event for school, a test, a job performance, or just meeting with family members and friends and trying to leave a good impression, everyone is familiar with the idea of having to do a good job and having a lot to prove.

It can be hard to perform well when you know that so much is riding on your shoulders. It can cause you to second-guess yourself, feel anxious and pressured, or, worse yet, actually make some mistakes that can complicate your life, your friendships, your job.

Now imagine that the decisions—and the mistakes— that you make are being watched by thousands of people, all of whom have a very vested interest in how well you do. Imagine that everyone is judging you and they are looking for you to succeed. If you don't, you're not just letting yourself down. You are letting thousands of people down.

That is a feeling that Chris Nicholl knows all too well. And a certain performance of his will forever highlight just how hard it is to perform in front of fans, and how painful it is to mess up and let them all down.

Soccer is an unforgiving sport, not just because it will push you and your body to its limits. But it's also unforgiving because the fans who cherish and follow it so closely are very devoted and when they feel disappointed by someone's performance, they often don't let it go.

Nicholl learned that the hard way back in March 1976.

There are multiple positions within each and every soccer team and the defender is one of the most important ones.[1] The defender, as you would imagine, defends their team's goal and gives a lot of help to the goalie, preventing the ball from even coming close to the netting of the goal.

Sometimes the defender is the last, best hope against being scored upon.

But did you know that usually around 10 percent of all goals are actually made by the defender against their very own team? This happens because we are all human and make mistakes. Sometimes a player will be trying to hit the ball with their head in one direction, only for it to go in the opposite way from the one planned. All sports are an imperfect science and these sorts of mishaps happen.

But for Chris Nicholl, it happened multiple times all in the span of just one game.

Nicholl was a defender for Aston Villa back in the 70s and was playing against Leicester City in March of 1976. The game took place at Filbert Street and was tied 2–2 after a tough game. And Nicholl ultimately scored each and every single goal.

Can you believe that? Can you believe how horrible he felt? Nichol managed to score all four goals, two with his head and two with his feet.

Brian Alderson of Leicester City put up the first assist about 15 minutes into the game, and the diligent Nicholl headed it sharply into his own goal. Oops, that was the first mistake.

The defender clearly did a lot of introspection and felt inner turmoil throughout the following 25 minutes. He appeared to have made amends with himself and was playing better when, in the 40th minute, he scored an equalizer by taking advantage of a mix-up involving Brian Little's header in the Leicester penalty area.

Both goals by Nicholl put the sides at a 1–1 tie going into halftime.

The madness continued after that.

Frank Worthington of the home squad floated across into the penalty area in the second half. Bob Lee, a forward, lunged for the header while being intently watched by Nicholl. The Irishman ultimately won the ball, throwing in another magnificent header that soared past a now perplexed Burridge and into the goal.

Nicholl now had a sort of hat-trick and Leicester City was up 2–1. As the battle raged on, the home team maintained its lead for the final four minutes or so of play. Aston Villa exerted significant pressure, earning a corner. A commotion resulted after Chico Hamilton floated the kick. Nicholl kicked the ball in again amid the chaos to make it 2–2. And that would be the final score, thanks to the hard work—and major mistakes—of Nicholl.

In the end, Aston Villa scored twice on kicks, while Leicester City scored twice on headers. The symmetry from Nicholl was astounding.

The fans were, understandably, pretty unhappy with how everything had happened during that game. But, at the same time, they were slightly amazed by what Nicholl did. It's not every day that one player scores four goals, especially two against his own team. So the fans watching that day were displeased and let Nicholl know it. But they were also stunned to be a part of soccer history and shocked by just how odd the entire match was.

As for Nicholl, he took it all in stride. Of course, he was very hard on himself during the game and immediately after. He was beating himself up because he knew that he had cost his team a victory. If only he had scored all four points for *his* team, instead of two for them and two for his opponents.

But as time went on, Nicholl became a lot more gentle with himself and would later look back on the match with a great sense of humor. He was actually quite proud of what he had done that day.

In fact, at the end of the match, Nicholl came to the ref and asked if he would be able to take the ball home as a token of the historic, bizarre, one-of-a-kind day. But the referee said no.[2] It didn't matter; Nicholl knew that he had already cemented his status as a soccer player who had done something not only unlikely and rare, but also ultimately incredibly bizarre too.

It is good that he didn't beat himself up too much because the game didn't truly matter too much in the grand scheme of things. Were the fans upset? Yes, they were. But they got over it and there were plenty of other games for them to pay attention to and devote themselves to. As for Nicholl, he would go on to have a long and successful career and this match where he scored four points, two for his team and two of the other, was just a footnote of his tenure on the field.[3]

This one of a kind game is a prime example of how soccer, perhaps more than any other sport, is really a game of a bunch of people and a ball, nothing more and nothing less. There is very little equipment, the rules are fairly simple and easy to follow, and the real heart and soul of the game is just two groups of players attempting to take hold and control the ball and score for their team.

Because soccer really is a game of people and a soccer ball, mistakes like this are going to happen. No one is perfect, accidents occur all the time, especially with a sport that is so simple and wonderfully primitive like this one. Now, that being said, it's not often that someone will score two points for both teams. That rarely ever happens.

While the fans might have been upset and Nicholl himself might have been extra hard on himself for a moment, everyone knew they had all been a part of something special during that wild and crazy game.

6

IT'S NOT OVER TILL THE WHISTLE BLOWS

E ven if you're not a soccer expert who has studied the game for years, you know that each and every game can be decided by a single point. That is why each and every possession is so very important. You have to pretend that every time you touch the ball will be the most important and can be a deciding factor in either your success or failure.

This is why you see so many soccer players who pour their hearts out on the field. They play hard and they don't let up the tempo, not even as the game is almost over. One goal can change it all and that goal can be scored in only a matter of seconds. You can never give up, not until the final whistle blows.

But what happens if that whistle isn't heard? What happens if a physical mishap prevents the official from actually sounding the whistle and ending the match? What happens then?

Being a referee can be a great and rewarding job but you need to be able to withstand a lot of pressure, a lot of distrust and anger from fans—and players and coaches—and you need to enter each and every game with a thick skin or else you simply will not be able to take it. Refereeing games is simply not for everyone because of these prerequisites.

Fans have gotten so involved and fired up about soccer that they have actually killed referees in certain parts of the world because of the decisions they made.[1] But thankfully there are some mistakes that are a lot more fun—and funnier—than that.

Let's take a look back at a famous—or, rather, infamous —soccer game from April 1960, when a certain referee's faulty teeth caused a whole lot of ruckus on the field.

The two teams, Norager and Ebeltoft, were at odds and fighting it out on the soccer field.[2] Things were incredibly tight for the entire game, but as the game was coming to an end, it looked like one team was pulling ahead of the other and victory was in sight.

There were only a few seconds left in the game, and Norager was ahead 4–3. They just needed to hold on for the last moment of the game and then they would be able to claim a huge win that would have the fans dancing in the stands and the players celebrating on the field.

That is when things got incredibly odd, unique, and just straight-up hilarious.

The final seconds had come and gone and it was time for the match to conclude. But when referee Henning Erikstrup raised his whistle to his lips, the worst possible and most unlikely outcome happened.

Erikstrup's false teeth, his dentures, chose that moment to slip loose of the grip on his gums and come tumbling out. Because his teeth fell out of his jaws to the ground, Erikstrup's whistle was not very loud. It was a mere whisper instead of a loud, engaging blow. It was so low, in fact, that the Ebeltoft players didn't know and kept moving happily toward the opposition's goal. They thought they could still claim a big win as long as they made the next goal.

And guess what? That's exactly what they did. Completely unaware that the ref had attempted to end the game, the Ebeltoft team raced down the field, shot the ball with speed and authority, and scored a dramatic goal to even the score at 4–4. It was a tie game, a draw. As expected, the team and their loyal fans went wild, thinking that they had secured a tie when defeat seemed inevitable.

The festivities got underway immediately and people were elated with the results of the competition. They had earned a draw and Ebeltoft was elated. However, these feelings of elations would all be stripped away from the team.

Erikstrup, who didn't appear shamed by his misfortune and stood by his call, drew attention to his error by claiming that Ebeltoft's goal wasn't valid because he had already planned to sound the final whistle. Both teams were shocked, although one was much happier than the other, of course. They were bewildered by the fact that the game was apparently over when the last goal was made. No whistle was heard but, according to the ref, that didn't matter. His intent was to end the game but his dentures fell out. But his intent mattered more than anything else. And Ebeltoft lost the game.

As you can imagine, people were livid. Fans of the losing team were up in arms and said that since a whistle wasn't blown, the last goal should still count. The game was still going, they cried out. Dentures or no dentures, a whistle wasn't heard, so technically the game was still playing, right?

Considerable debate and some intense words and tempers surrounded everyone at that moment. There were discussions about overturning the call and letting the game end in a draw. But Erikstrup wouldn't budge on this decision and the 4–3 victory was given to Norager.

Ebeltoft, naturally incensed, objected to the outcome. To ensure that their argument was heard, they presented it to the Danish Football Association. They were going to fight for their victory as long as possible and they were going to devote a lot of energy to overturning the call that was impacted by a set of false teeth.

However, the Danish FA stood by their dentally impaired official, allowing Norager to keep their incredibly lucky victory.

You can bet that many wild events have happened during soccer games but this surely takes the cake. You would be hard-pressed to find another game in which the conclusion wasn't properly called because teeth had fallen out. Soccer has seen a lot of wild and crazy moments, but few have even come close to this.

But if you want to talk about a moment when a referee *did* decide that he had made a mistake, go no further than February 2006. The game was between

Peterborough North End and Royal Mail AYL and it involved a ref named Andy Wain.

During the game, North End goalie Richard McGaffin was upset about a goal that put his opponents up 2–1. And he was letting his opinion be known loudly and without any restraint.

The referee immediately lost his temper and started acting no better than an incensed player. We have all seen players who have fought on the field in a melee of fists and anger, and Andy Wain was about to outdo them all.

Wain strode across the field and was about to clash with the goalie. He untucked his shirt, he pressed his face against the player's and, for a moment, it looked like there was about to be a physical fight.

But cooler heads prevailed and Wain quickly got himself under control. He would later admit that he had been going through some personal problems at home during the time and that had an impact on his temper during the match.

A man of honor, Wain did what any good ref would: he gave himself a red card and ejected himself from the field.[3] The players and fans sat dumbfounded as the entire event went down. From a near-fight to an ejected ref, that game had a couple of things that were rarely ever seen.

From faulty teeth to fuming tempers, referees can sometimes get involved in soccer games for reasons they'd rather avoid. No one will ever say that they aren't a vital part of the game—and they are all human just like the rest of us. That is what leads to memorable and unique moments like the ones we just talked about. And these moments are only possible on the soccer field.

7

THE STRANGEST TRANSFER PAYMENTS EVER

I n the game of soccer, certain teams are willing to pay a whole lot of money to get the players they think will work best for them.

And as time has gone on, the amount of money that is spent on the acquisitions, known as "transfer payments," have gotten exceedingly large. Even yesterday's large amounts seem tiny compared to just how much teams will pay today to land the player of their dreams.

For example, Neymar's transfer was 222 million euros in 2017, which is a massive sum of money.[1] While it is really hard to wrap your head around that amount, there are other terms to certain transfers that are even more incredible—and hard to believe. These teams aren't always spending money to get their players.

A transfer payment is a very complicated, confusing set of negotiations and payments that are really hard to understand if you aren't a soccer executive running a team. They are usually paid in installments because that amount of money can't be shelled out all at once. Remember, we are talking about hundreds of millions, not just a few thousand.

You have to remember all of the people involved in these sorts of trade. Not only do the players have to be communicated with but agents, team executives and others are all involved. That's a lot of cooks in one kitchen and many ways for it to go wrong.

And deep pockets are always required because there are transfer fees associated with these deals. That means that on top of the contract being created, soccer organizations also have to pay fees each time they sign a new star.

Transfers are not easy and they are not made overnight, and many of the details are never known to the fans who enjoy the game. But some catch the eye more than others because they are just so hard to believe. Yes, throughout the history of the game, some transfers have been rather wild, and so different that you have to see them to believe them.

Let's take a good, hard look at some of the most unique and extravagant transfer payments throughout soccer history.

Collins John would become one of the best players with Premier League team Fulham. But before he got there, he was an athlete signed to FC Twente. And when FC Twente had initially wooed John to their team, they found out that knowledge really is as good as money to some.

They were only able to acquire him from DES Nijverdal after they donated a set of encyclopedias to a local high school. In the grand scheme of things, that is a lot cheaper than spending millions upon millions on a player. But in a sense it is worth even more because knowledge is power and just think about how much knowledge is inside the pages of an encyclopedia.

Ion Radu's transfer payment was yet another interesting one that didn't rely solely on cold, hard cash. His team was having a tough time in the late 1990s so they decided to sell Radu away to another team.

And the chairman in charge of the transfer just asked for two tons of beef and pork instead of actual currency.[2] And guess what? He got exactly that. This shows that it's not always a check that is being written —sometimes it's a grocery list.

When Franco Di Santo was transferred to Audax Italian in Chile, he was acquired by the team giving up two goal nets, as well as more than 40 liters of paint. That was enough to get the deal done and send Di Santo on his way to his new team.

Back in the 1920s, English defender Ernie Blenkinsop was sent to a new team for the cool price of a barrel of beer on top of 100 pounds. The 100 pounds went to the team, but the beer was shared among Blenkinsop and his teammates. That sounds like a good deal for everyone involved.

There are so many examples of truly wild transfer payments throughout the history of the game. For example, Giuliano Grazioli was traded for three packets of chips and a Mars bar, and Hugh McLanahan was acquired with three full freezers of ice cream, while Ian Wright was sent to his new squad for a set of weights in a workout room.

But perhaps the oddest, hardest to believe transfer payment that has ever happened went down when Kenneth Kristensen was moving from Vindbjart to Floey. In order to acquire the transfer, Foley paid with a pile of fresh, succulent shrimp ready for eating.

Believe it or not, the massive haul of shrimp did the trick and Kristensen was well on his way to his new team.[3]

All of these crazy stories just show how seriously soccer teams take their stars. These fees and deals usually involve an awful lot of money changing hands. That is still the principal way that soccer organizations transfer their players and build their teams.

But sometimes they do things in an unorthodox way. Sometimes they will do whatever it takes, no matter how wild, in order to land the stars that they know can help them win. From pounds of shrimp, to meat, to beer and books, multiple soccer teams have done whatever it takes and have cobbled together the strangest assortments to find victory.

Now, imagine how you'd feel if you were a soccer player who got sent to a new team in exchange for nearly 200 pounds of fresh shrimp. Would you be flattered or offended?

8

GOALS GALORE!

A s in many sports, soccer players have become comfortable speaking their minds, letting their opinions be known, and never backing down from the conventional wisdom that tells them to just shut up and play the game.

When something upsets soccer players, they often let it be known. They will speak to their fellow teammates, their coaches, the press, and practically anyone who will listen.

And if they are truly upset about something that has happened, soccer players will take it upon themselves to raise their voices—even in the middle of the game.

Recently, there have been many athletes who have taken to the field to discuss some major and very important issues, such as human rights, inequality, equal pay for men and women, and more. While some people agree with their approach to speaking out, others find that the field is not the right place to protest.

FIFA president Gianni Infantino sure doesn't think so. Speaking about recent protests about human rights in Qatar, Infantino said that all players should "respect football" and not protest on the field because the fans don't want to pay attention to the world's problems during the game.[1] Instead, they want to focus on the game and *only* the game.

His lengthy quote is as follows:

> *"It's not about prohibiting or not prohibiting. It's about respecting regulations; we have regulations which say on the field of play, you play football, and that's what we did.*
> *Everyone is free to express his views, his opinion, his beliefs, the way he believes, as long as it's done in a respectful way.*
> *When it comes to the pitch, to the field of play, you need to respect football, you need to respect the field of play, and these regulations are exactly there for this reason. This is nothing new; they are there for this reason to respect and to protect the 211 football*

teams, not 211 heads of states, regimes, or what have you."

While some protests from soccer players have been about the most pressing matters of our time, others have been a lot less consequential. And sometimes when players have used their games as a chance to speak out about something they don't like, they have looked a bit silly.

There is no time when protests have been as shocking and unbelievable as the time in 2002 when one team let their anger be known by scoring against themselves. That's right—the team didn't even score against their opponents but instead conquered their own goal almost 150 times. That's quite a way to protest.

It all goes back to the THB Champions League in Madagascar in 2002.[2] Although it is a small island country, the people of Madagascar really love the game of soccer and much attention was being paid to each and every game to see who was going to win it all.

The scoreline was 2–2 in the second-to-last game between Stade Olympique l'Emyrne (SOE) and Domoina Soavina Atsimondrano (DSA).

But then it all changed because of one pivotal officiating call from the ref.

The referee, Benjamina Razafintsalama, gave SOE a penalty, ending their chances of gaining the upper hand. That was the end of the game and, really, the end of SOE's chances of becoming champions.

But the tournament went on, even though the outcome was a foregone conclusion at that point. Despite the low stakes, the final matchup pitted SOE against As Adema Analamanga. Yet, none of it even mattered at this point. However, Adema was now assured of winning the championship and SOE was assured of finishing in second place according to the way the tournament distributed scores for victories and draws.

So, some people were wondering what the point was. And they were very angry that things came to that point.

What followed next was perhaps one of the oddest and most surprising on-field protests to ever be witnessed in modern sports. A week later, SOE was getting ready to take on Adema in a game that really didn't mean anything. And the team—and its manager—were still very upset. So upset, in fact, that team manager Ratimandresy Ratsarazaka took matters into his own hands and decided that he was going to get his team to speak out and make their opinions known.

When the players on his team were able to get possession of the ball at the start of the game, they did something no one expected. They didn't take it down the field and attempt a goal. No, instead they simply turned around, went up to their own netting and scored. Yes, they scored against themselves as a form of protest against the officiating call just a week before.

But that wasn't the only goal they'd score against their own keeper. They continued to get a hold of the ball and then run it back to their very own goal. They scored again and again and again. In total they scored on their own goal 149 times. Yes, the score was 149 to 0.[3]

The other team just sat by and watched it all go down. What else were they supposed to do? The referees were a bit more upset but they only had so much control and so much ability to stop things. So in the end, the fans, the other team, and officiants pretty much just sat by and watched SOE score in their own goal nearly 150 times.

The league was more upset than the other team, the fans, and the refs combined. They were not happy watching a team mock their judgment call and then protest on the field in such an open and blatant way.

So the story didn't end with the 149–0 self-routing. Instead, just weeks later, the league punished SOE by taking away their second-place title, barring them from a tournament in the future, and even suspended some of the players for the rest of the year.

As for the coach who organized the entire protest, he was suspended for a whopping three years for coming up with the idea and making it happen.

As for the fans, they grew upset. They had paid their good, hard-earned cash to watch a soccer game and instead watched a group of men just continually score their own goal as a way to push back against the league. They demanded their money back and they bad-mouthed SOE for a long time after that.

Years later, some of the players on the team would say they should have gone about things in a different way. They regretted what they did to the fans and they openly acknowledged that it was a poor thing to do.

No matter how they feel about it now, no one can deny that this once in a lifetime game was one for the record books. It ended in a lot of angry feelings and some suspensions, but it definitely got a point across.

The game of soccer can be used for good and if players are truly moved to speak out against something that is negatively affecting the world, they will do just that. In the years ahead, it shouldn't be surprising to see many more players speak out and step out onto the field and spout their beliefs about a number of things.

But they should be careful about what their causes are. If they are fighting for the rights of humans across the globe, that will probably be considered a good thing. But if they are simply speaking out about a referee call that they disagree with, they need to make sure they are being careful not to alienate their fans and make themselves look even worse.

There is a time and place for protesting but players need to think long and hard about when they do. Otherwise, they will do themselves—and the rest of the world—more harm than good. This iconic and bizarre protest from the field is clear proof of that.

9

HAT TRICKS AREN'T ENOUGH FOR RONALDO

"If you think you are already perfect, then you never will be."

— CRISTIANO RONALDO

A s we have discussed before, it is hard to score a goal in the game of soccer. The skill and speed and determination needed to make it happen can seem downright impossible to acquire at any given time.

That is even more true when you are talking about a professional soccer match. These games aren't like the ones that you see in the school yard. Instead, they are much harder, much more intense, with many more fans and so much more on the line. The tensions are higher and so is the difficulty level.

Now, imagine scoring a goal not just once during a pro soccer match. And imagine scoring not just two or three times. Imagine having the downright amazing skill to be able to score five times in one game. It sounds impossible because, for many people, it pretty much is. Most people are not able to read a field, team-mates and opponents well enough to score that many times in one game.

But, then again, most people are not Ronaldo. He's known as one of the best soccer players of all time and one of the reasons for that is because he is the only player in history to score five goals in one game—twice. Five goals in one game two times during his career—that is quite a feat, one that has quite literally never been duplicated.

The intensity of the game and the hard-fought determination of the opponents didn't matter to Ronaldo. He was still able to make history multiple times. That just goes to show how special he is.

Real Madrid is a soccer team that seems destined to make superstars. Throughout their history, there have been many icons who have suited up and worn their cleats for the team. But few have had the global impact of Ronaldo, who has reached billions of people and set multiple records.

When you look back through Real Madrid's history, you will find that they have actually had seven players who have scored five goals in a single game. Yes, Ronaldo was not the first. But he did so much more than simply achieving that mammoth accomplishment. He also reached 300 goals for Real Madrid. In fact, he did that during one of the games in which he scored his five goals.

Ronaldo had this first epic accomplishment in a match against Granada, in which he scored his first goal after about thirty minutes, and then finished his hat trick within eight minutes of that. He scored two more goals in the second half of that game, leaving the fans both stunned and speechless.[1]

Ronaldo was on fire that season, when he scored six hat tricks throughout the year.

But his streak of scoring five goals in a single game continued a few months later when he put up another five against Espanyol, adding to the final score of 6–0 for Real Madrid.[2]

Each and every time Ronaldo scored a goal, his followers went absolutely wild. They did this not only because they supported the star but because they also knew that he was perhaps about to score another five goals or create some other piece of history. That was just the way that he played—he was at a level that so few other soccer stars ever get to.

During his career, Ronaldo was seen as one of the best soccer players in the world—if not the very best. What was it about Cristiano Ronaldo that made him so special?

People talk a lot about the dynamism of his position He is fast, sometimes downright unstoppable. He plays with a sort of speed that is hard to keep up with and many competitors have tried—and failed—to slow him down. Even as he got older, he was able to keep his body in the sort of shape that allowed him to move with lightning-fast efficiency and speed throughout an entire match on the field.

His shooting was also second-to-none when he was at his peak.[3] Even several years after being a rookie star, Ronaldo was scoring more than anyone else on his team and many other soccer players, even those who were much younger than him.

He is also known for being excellent when it comes to working alongside his teammates. He has been called out at times for being selfish but Ronaldo has put a lot of energy and effort into making sure he is more of a team player and now has a mentality that puts his squad above himself.

Ronaldo is easily one of the best to ever take to the field and it's not just because he has won so many games and gotten far in the World Cup. Instead, Ronaldo's greatness can be found in the ways that he brings his team together, keeps his head in the game, and breaks records for the franchise he plays for.

Scoring five goals in a single game is something that so few people have done. It is wildly impressive and there is no denying that. But doing the feat twice puts Ronaldo in a league that is really head and shoulders above the rest of soccer players in the world.

10

URUGUAY RISES TO CONQUER THE WORLD CUP

When you think about the World Cup today, you think of the literally billions of people who watch every game, the massive amount of advertising, the new stories, parades, and so much more.

Indeed, the World Cup is now such a large event that the entire globe seems to stop and pay attention when it comes around every four years. But it wasn't always that way.

Did you know that the World Cup is less than 100 years old? Something this big and this successful and this captivating seems like it has been around since the invention of soccer but it was actually started back in 1930. And when it started, it wasn't even close to the size it is today. Back then, many people didn't know about the World Cup and many nations didn't even send a team to participate in it.

Today, nearly every country will try to be a part of the World Cup and billions of dollars are generated by the interest in the games. But the first World Cup was wildly different and so much smaller, which definitely helped the first championship team, hailing from Uruguay.

The initial World Cup was actually held in that country and many people assumed they were gaining some home court benefits because of hosting the games. At that time, there were only 13 participants in the World Cup, far less than what we see today.[1] And Uruguay got off to a great start in the game, taking down Peru and Romania, before facing off against the United States, who they easily beat 6–1.

In that first World Cup Final, Uruguay had to square off against Argentina. Thanks to the hard work of players like Jose Cea, Santos Iriarte, Pablo Dorado, Hector Castro, and others, the Uruguay team ended up winning the first World Cup in a huge 4–2 victory.

This was a celebrated win, but one that paled in comparison to the intense competitions that would come in the future. It would be a few years before the World Cup was the sort of event that it is today. And although Uruguay was the first host and first victor, it would be 20 years before they would get another good shot at taking the top prize.

It is that victory that is still talked about today by many soccer fans all over the world.

By the time the 1950 World Cup rolled around, there were far more people paying attention. The games were growing in popularity, but they still had a long way to go before they were the world-stopping event that they are now.

The 1950 games were held in the neighboring country of Brazil and Uruguay felt very good about their chances of going far in the Cup.

Ironically, there were still only 13 teams participating in the World Cup at the time, but it wasn't due to lack of popularity of the games. Instead, there were many countries that were banned or refused to play in response to World War II, which had obviously ended only five years before.

In fact, the 1950 games were the first World Cup since 1938 as the war had made it impossible.

Bolivia was Uruguay's first opponent and they took them down with total ease, 8–0, to advance to the final stage of the World Cup. During this time, there wasn't a knockout round of the games, making it far easier to reach the final round but also tougher in some ways because every team knew they had a better chance of going far, if only they fought harder.

The final round had a round-robin schedule which meant that Uruguay would have a lot of games to get through to claim victory over the rest of the countries.

In the final group of four, Brazil beat Spain and Sweden, while Uruguay drew in a game against Spain and defeated Sweden. Heading into the final round, Brazil had four points collected while Uruguay had only three. That meant that Brazil just needed a draw to win the entire World Cup.

Yes, the cards seemed stacked against Uruguay at the time. Brazil was on their home court and the legion of fans had come out to cheer for their squad. Newspapers and the media were practically handing the trophy to Brazil before the game even started. And Uruguay knew that most everyone assumed they'd lose. In fact, the president of FIFA had already written a speech congratulating Brazil not only for hosting the games but also for winning the top prize.[2]

If that wasn't bad enough, Uruguay really was in the lions' den because they were playing against Brazil in Brazil. As you can imagine, people came out in droves and the cheering from the crowd for Brazil was downright deafening. The game wasn't going to start until 3 PM but the entire stadium was already completely filled by 11 AM, four hours before kickoff.

The Wall Street Journal perfectly summed up the scene:

> *"Millions of fans had flooded the streets of Rio de Janeiro's northern neighbourhoods, surrounding the Estadio Mario Filho, better known as the Maracanã... The luckiest 200,000 among them had been allowed inside... They had smuggled in streamers and flares and drums. Carnival on the terraces. For hours, they danced and sang in the sun, long before a single player took the field. They had all come to Brazil's new cathedral to soccer, purpose-built for this 1950 World Cup, to bask in their country's proudest moment. Brazil was about to beat Uruguay and win its first World Cup. They knew it."*

Uruguay was facing that sort of environment and yet they still weren't giving up the dream of winning their second World Cup tournament.

Unfortunately, at first it seemed like those dreams would be dashed and all the predictions would come true. It looked like Brazil was going to win the game after a whopping 17 goal attempts during the first 37 minutes of the game. Then, right before the 50-minute mark, Brazil scored their first goal and were well on their way to hoisting the trophy above their heads.

After that first goal, Uruguay challenged and the whole game was held up as the referees decided what to do. The goal ended up standing and that only fired up the Uruguay team even more, making them more determined to sink a goal and even the score.

Then, 66 minutes into the match, it happened. Alcides Ghiggia was able to find Juan Alberto Schiaffino, who sent the ball flying into the net and evened the score 1–1 for both teams.

The massive stadium seemingly full of only Brazil fans fell silent. They didn't expect this and they thought their team was well on its way to winning it all. For years, they had been waiting for Brazil to win the Cup and they had gotten so close. Now was it all on the verge of being taken away?

It was, because Uruguay wasn't slowing down. Just a few moments later, they scored yet another goal with just 11 minutes to go before the game was done. Ghiggia was again ready to find success for his team and was the one who got the ball into the goal.

Now the fans were screaming, crying out, pleading with Brazil to score again and tie up the game. But

Brazil couldn't meet their followers' demands and they lost the game. Uruguay, against all odds and the desires of thousands of people surrounding them, were able to beat the odds—and Brazil—to claim their second World Cup victory.

The country of Brazil did not handle their defeat well. There were reports of people collapsing in the streets, deaths, and some violence among citizens.[3] And the coach of the team allegedly exited the arena dressed as a nanny as a way to avoid the onslaught and disdain from the thousands of Brazilian fans who had just had their hearts broken.

As for Brazil's goalkeeper, Barbosa, he suffered a fate that was truly painful. He was punished by the public and soccer fans throughout the country. He was avoided, shunned, and literally hated by many people. In fact, things were so bad that he was denied a job as a soccer presenter years later in 1993. In Brazil, they took the failure very seriously, perhaps *too* seriously.

As for Uruguay, they were elated with the results of the game. Everyone had counted them out. As mentioned, things were so bad that speeches were already being written about Brazil's victory. But it was Uruguay who got the last laugh, and the trophy. The country was beside itself with joy, and a bit of shock, because they too had started to believe they wouldn't be able to win it all. But the faith of the fans and the strength of the team made the impossible truly possible during the still-famous 1950 World Cup.

Since then, Uruguay has not been able to repeat their success and these two victories are the only ones that the country has received. Although the nation would love to add more victories to their record, they are happy knowing that they won both the first World Cup and another that no one thought they would.

11

THE BATTLE OF SANTIAGO

"I wasn't reffing a football match, I was acting as an umpire in military maneuvers."

— KEN ASHTON, ENGLISH REFEREE

Sadly, we are all aware that tensions sometimes rise incredibly high during a sports match. We have all heard and seen the many times when fans get too wild, too fired up, and start to attack one another as a way of fighting on behalf of their team. It is never a wise idea and it really makes all sports fans look bad.

But there are times when the tempers flaring belong to more than just the fans. In fact, there have been times when players, coaches and team staff members have gotten into fights, including very explosive ones.

What happens when two teams really don't like one another? What happens when outside events interfere with a game and make people feel on edge, angry, and ready to come to blows? Even the most professional and most-watched games are not immune from this sort of thing. And during one major World Cup game, tensions rose so much that the police were called. No, they weren't called on the fans watching. Instead, they were called to split up players on the field.

One soccer game is now so infamous that before it was broadcast on TV, BBC presenter David Coleman said, "Good evening. The game you are about to see is the most stupid, appalling, disgusting, and disgraceful exhibition of football, possibly in the history of football."

What led to such a nightmare of a game? What made this game more of a melee than an actual soccer match?

The year was 1962 and a lot of attention was being paid to the World Cup. All of Earth was still recovering from World War II. The World Cup had taken a hiatus during the war but it had established itself again when the war came to a close. During the decade that followed, Europe had hosted both of the World Cups. There were many people crying out for the games to be held in North or South America, as millions of fans hailed from that part of the world.

Sure enough, Chile was selected to host the games in 1962 and the fans couldn't be more excited. Because of the attention being paid to the country, hundreds of journalists from all over the world flooded to Chile to write about the nation for legions of soccer-adoring fans back home.

Two of those journalists, Antonio Ghirardelli and Corrado Pizzinelli from Italy, set off a chain of events that would tarnish their reputations and the reputation of the World Cup for years to come.

Writing about the Chilean capital of Santiago, these two writers didn't cast a favorable light on the nation that was about to host the games. In fact, they wrote that the city of Santiago was "A poverty-stricken dump full of crime and loose women."

As you can imagine, the citizens of Chile were enraged at not just the journalists but also the people of Italy and, especially, the players who were on the Italian soccer team.[1] And they let them know it. The country was immediately ready for blood and eager to strike back against the writers and the entire country that they hailed from.[2]

Things got even worse when Chile was set to face off against Italy in a game that would determine which squad would move forward. The thought of those two teams—with all their angry feelings brewing—playing against one another set millions of people and soccer fans on edge.

English referee Ken Aston was tasked with officiating the game and he knew right away that it was going to be the toughest job of his life. Even before the first whistle blew, players from both the Chilean and Italian teams had actually spit on one another.

But then the game started, and the hope was that the two sides would be able to remain professional and respect the game that they were there to play.

Those hopes were quickly dashed.

Twelve minutes into the game, Italian player Giorgio Ferrini was steamed about what he considered a foul and so he tried to attack Honorino Landa of Chile by kicking him. Aston wasn't having it and immediately ejected the player, but it would take eight more minutes and a group of police officers to get the Italian star off the field.

If you thought that was bad, things were only going to get worse as the match went on.

Right before halftime, Chile's Leonel Sanchez was fouled by Mario David. Sanchez wasn't just a soccer player; he was the son of a boxer and he responded like a boxer would, instantly finding the man who fouled him and hitting him in the face with a left hook.

That was all missed by the refs but it certainly wasn't missed by David, who was left reeling. Just a few minutes later, he kicked Sanchez in the face before being kicked out of the game.

This meant that Italy only had 9 players on the field against Chile's 11.

Police were called onto the field several more times during the game as it was quickly devolving into an all-out fight between both sides. The tensions were rising in the crowd too, which was booing the Italian squad and cheering on each and every violent move from the Chilean guys.

At the end of the day, this *was* still a soccer match and goals were being scored, between the repeated police interventions and the fights on the field. In the end, the Italians were beaten 2–0 and they were also given a bad rap by the local press, who said they were to blame for all of the violence on the field.

After that game, Italy went on to win against Switzerland but had already been eliminated because of

West Germany's win over Chile just one day before that. As for Chile, they would go on to end the tournament in third place, which remains the best finish for that team in World Cup history.[3]

Both teams looked bad leaving the game and while the immediate media coverage blamed Italy for the fighting, Chile would also look bad in the eyes of many, especially as the years went on. Today, the game is considered one of the low points in World Cup history because of the sheer nastiness that was seen on the field. These were a group of professional players who were supposed to put their differences aside for the good of the game and the fans who were rooting for them. But in the end, they looked no better than a group of men duking it out in a barroom after a night of heavy drinking.

As for the ref, Ken Aston, he probably made out worse than anyone else during that game. Not only did he have to put up a fight to keep things as civil as possible, but he also strained his Achilles tendon during the game and didn't get to ref another game in the Cup that year.[4]

It would take a few days before the rest of the world would see the game, since footage traveled slowly during that time. When the news finally did showcase the game to those beyond Chile, millions of people shook their heads and then demanded more of the athletes they were supporting.

12

SOCCER'S WORST INJURY

A ccidents happen often in life. Because of that, injuries happen often too. And while most injuries are able to be taken care of quickly, some are really detrimental, painful, and downright gruesome and hard to look at.

Soccer has sadly had a lot of experience with some nasty injuries over the years. The game doesn't give a lot of protection to the players on the field. Aside from shin guards and a well-placed cup in the shorts, there isn't much standing between the players and some serious damage to their bodies.

It's hard to figure out the worst soccer injury of all time but we do know there are many that have captured the attention of fans, and not for the best reasons. Like a train wreck, it has been hard to look away from these painful and awful soccer injuries.

The sad truth is that there is no way to completely avoid soccer injuries. Because of the use of feet and legs, there are going to be a lot of bumps, bruises, and broken bones at times. The most common injuries occurring because of soccer include damage to the ankles, knees and calves, but there are so many more ways that a player can be damaged—sometimes permanently—when they are trying to get ahold of the soccer ball.

Hold on tight and prepare yourself because we are going to discuss the worst soccer injuries that have ever happened. Brace yourself.

In 2008, Eduardo Da Silva suffered a nasty injury that still makes people cringe and shiver with disgust today. He broke his left fibula and dislocated his left ankle after a rough tackle. The injuries were brutal to watch and tough to look at afterwards. They also took a very long time to recover from.

In fact, it was more than a year before Da Silva felt like his old self.

Yet, that was just one of many painful and rough injuries that have befallen soccer players over the years. In 2007, Kieron Dyer suffered not one but two leg fractures. His right leg was shattered in two different places above the knee and he was immediately carted off the field and sent to the hospital via ambulance.[1]

If you don't like seeing body parts being twisted around, then you should never watch the footage of Francesco Totti from 2006. The captain of his team, Totti suffered a very intense serious leg injury that resulted in him twisting his left ankle. It was so bad that he couldn't even stand and was taken off the field in a stretcher.[2]

Danish player Jacob Olesen nearly caused some people to faint in October 2006 because of a gruesome injury he suffered on the field. The dislocation of his left ankle was so severe that it looked to be literally hanging by a thread from his body. Screaming on the field after the dislocation, Olesen was in shock and could hardly believe the sight of his foot seemingly turned around from the position it should be in.

It would be six months before he would be able to use that foot again. Honestly, he was lucky it only took that long as some people would never walk again after a dislocation like that.

Ewald Lienen was a soccer player from the 1980s who is known best for his amazing skills as well as a truly horrendous incident that left him bleeding and cut wide open on the field. In August 1981, his thigh was slit open by the studs of another player's cleats. The deep wound was so intense that muscle and femur were exposed and visible to people watching the game. It looked like a scene out of an emergency room.

Believe it or not, Lienen was able to get up and run over to the coach of the other team, blaming him for the damage to his body. But that was the end of the game for Lienen, who needed 23 stitches to be sealed back up.[3]

If you want to touch upon what is considered perhaps the worst soccer injury of all time, then you need to discuss Davis Busst's. It is one that soccer fans—and especially soccer players—still think about today, like a nightmare that is impossible to erase from the brain.

In 1996, Busst was playing a match at Old Trafford. When Busst smashed into Manchester United player Densi Irwin, the bone of his leg literally pierced the skin and blood was seen flowing directly onto the grass of the field.

Both Busst's tibia and fibula were fractured and the gruesome moment was caught by cameras and was viewed by thousands of people who were rooting for the teams on from the stands. The entire crowd became totally silent as they waited to see what was going to happen to Busst. Sadly, he would never be able to play professionally again because of the damage done to his body.

Because of the severity of the injury, the bloodshed on the field, and the impact it had on his life, Busst's injury is still talked about as something infamous, historic, and terrifying.

Soccer isn't an easy game and it comes with a lot of challenges and, sadly, dangers. But the injuries we just discussed are the worst of the worst. Because of them, some people have said that soccer players should have more protection to keep them safe. But the people least likely to plead for that are soccer players themselves, who are willing to keep playing despite the risks.

Soccer isn't an easy or painless sport and these horrendous injuries prove that.

A NOTE TO READERS

At this point, we hope that you have already learned a lot about the magical, world-changing game of soccer. Hopefully you have seen that this game, started as an offshoot of rugby, has become so much more.

Indeed, a sport as important and impactful as soccer needs more awareness. People should know that it is more than just a game. In fact, it is a way of life. Of all the sports in the world, few have touched the hearts of as many people as soccer.

What better way to spread the word about the power of this sport and the amazing stories from its history than for more readers to enjoy this book? The whole goal of this book was to spread the word about soccer, to inspire people to learn even more and follow the sport that has touched the hearts of so many people.

A great way to get more people to read our book is to write a review about it. It won't take you much time and it surely isn't that hard, but it can do an awful lot for the future of the book and the audience it finds.

When you write a review about this book on Amazon, Google, or any other website, what does it do? It will allow more people to see the book. Search results will bring the book up and the good review will get them more interested.

You don't have to write much either! It won't take much time and it'll work wonders for the future of the book and, really, the awareness of soccer and all that it has done.

I really appreciate you reading this book so far and I promise there are so many great stories ahead about the history of the game and its impact on the world. But if you have a few minutes, do me a huge favor and hop on Amazon and let the world know all that this book has taught you!

And with that out of the way, let's head into the next stories about soccer and its meaningful effect on the world of sports.

Leave your review with this QR code

13

THE GAME OF THE CENTURY

P laying professional soccer is hard enough. There is so much on the line and each and every victory is taken seriously by millions of fans and the players on the field.

But nothing is more intense with more pressure than playing in the World Cup. It truly is the best of the best when it comes to soccer games. Those who are able to claim victory in the World Cup are celebrated forever, while those who fall short are shunned and often despised by the fans who were once cheering them on.

However, if that isn't bad enough, playing the World Cup at a high elevation is the worst of all. That is because the higher the elevation of the field, the harder it is to breathe and, therefore, run and compete in the game. There have been many people who have grown sick and injured because of a lack of ample oxygen. It's not only hard to play a sport in a high elevation area, it's actually downright dangerous.

The 1970 World Cup Semifinal is a great example of this. Held in Mexico City, it required all players to take time to adjust and prepare for a high-stakes game. But few things could really prepare them for the game and the tension that came with it.

The 1970 World Cup was a chance for two well-known and celebrated teams to match up and see who would come out on top. The two-time world champions Italy were going to square off against the 1954 winners West Germany.

The lead-up to their battle was massive and intense. More than 30 million people back in Italy watched as their team was able to pull out a win, even though the game was being held at 2 AM local time because of the time difference. Prior to the match against West Germany, Italy wasn't actually doing that many amazing things. In fact, they only scored a single goal in three games. As for West Germany, they were flexing their strength a lot more before meeting Italy and had scored ten goals in their previous three games.

Therefore, coming into the game, it was assumed that Italy was the underdog team and they would have to show something they hadn't before if they wished to conquer West Germany. Right off the bat, it seemed like they might do just that. It took Italy only eight minutes to score the first goal of the match.

Players and coaches would later admit that it took some time for everyone to adjust to the high elevation of Mexico City. For fans watching at home, it didn't appear as if any adjustment was necessary as both teams were racing up and down the field with speed and power as if they weren't having trouble breathing. However, those involved said they felt increasingly tired and sluggish and were fighting against their own bodies.

After that first initial goal by Italy, not a lot happened on the field. For the next 80-plus minutes, nothing challenged Italy's 1–0 lead. But that changed during injury time at the end of the second half, when Karl-Heinz Schnellinger of West Germany scored a goal. Fans cheered on as the game was tied and few people knew what would happen next.

What occurred after that second goal is the reason why many people called it the Game of the Century.

All the players were feeling winded, wiped out, and were having trouble moving forward. But they knew what was on the line. With tired legs and a body that wanted to give up, West Germany's Muller scored a goal at 94 minutes, giving his team their first lead of the game.

But that goal was met by another from Italy just four minutes later. After more than 90 minutes, both teams were now fired up and ready to leave it all on the field, despite the screaming protests from their bodies. Again, the game was tied and fans were downright foaming at the mouth as both sides of the field were panting, gasping to inhale what little air there was at such an elevation.

As intense and back-and-forth as the game was to that point, it wasn't over yet. In fact, it wasn't over by a long shot.

Extra time in this match was when history was made. For the first time in a World Cup game, there were five goals scored during the extra period of play, which is still a record to this day.

Despite the elevation, despite the long game, despite the exhaustion of both teams, they were still able to duke it out and battle hard for the entirety of the game, and then some.

14

WOMEN SETTING THE STANDARDS IN SOCCER

Today, most soccer fans can name numerous huge female players. Over the last few decades, women have dominated the sport in many ways, just like they have found great success in other sports such as basketball, tennis, golf, and even racing.

Soccer was sadly late in the game when it came to allowing women to thrive. While the first men's World Cup occurred back in 1930, it wasn't until 1991 that the sport caught up with the times and allowed women their own World Cup as well.

And since then, multiple female stars have risen through the ranks, changed the game, and inspired millions of young girls across the world to dive head-first into the sport they all love so much.

Believe it or not, there were women soccer clubs more than 100 years ago. Back in the 1890s, some of the most popular clubs in London were women's clubs. In fact, games with only female players were gaining in popularity for all types of fans. There were games that featured only women stars that attracted more than 10,000 people in the stands, even way back then.

The biggest crowd in the early days of female soccer wasn't until the year 1920. It was then that the Dick, Kerr Ladies team played against the St. Helen's Ladies squad on Boxing Day, December 26.[1] That match was a huge draw and brought more than 53,000 fans to the stands.

It was clear that soccer with female athletes had struck a chord and had made thousands, if not millions, of young fans. But that didn't mean that the old-fashioned, deeply held beliefs of those in power were suddenly going to change.

You have to remember that back then, women just didn't have a place at the table like they do in the modern world. They didn't work with men, they didn't vote like men, they didn't hold any sort of power like men. And the Football Association that was running all of soccer at the time wasn't going to bring equality to their game. Therefore, the Association actually banned women's football games and leagues.[2]

This deeply held belief was firm and seemingly unchanging. Therefore, the days of women in soccer came to an end back in the 20s, and it would be a very long time until things altered and the most popular sport on earth caught up with the changing opinions and viewpoints of the rest of the world.

In fact, it wasn't until the 1960s, some 40 years later, that women were able to play in professional soccer.

In the year 1969, the Women's Football Association, or WFA, was formed. And right away, the inclusion of women in soccer garnered a very strong response from the fans who had been waiting literally decades to see females on the field again. In fact, just three years later, the first Women's FA Cup Final was held in England and attracted a lot of attention.

For years, women's soccer teams made a lot of fans and it was obvious that it was having a huge impact. That's because there were more and more young women who were entering the sport after seeing their heroines rise through the ranks to find success and spread the word about soccer to others.

At the turn of the century, women's soccer was more popular than ever before. In the early 2000s, the American-led female team brought the sport to millions more fans, known for their successful record, their colorful players, and the way that the national media gave them much attention and celebration.

But it would be years later that women's soccer had perhaps its most memorable game of all time.

The year was 2011 and the teams from Brazil and the United States were set to face off against one another.[3]

At the time, the US team came into the World Cup as the top team on Earth, the number one team throughout the sport, but Brazil wasn't going to go down without a strong fight. The two teams were set to face off against each other in the quarterfinal round but it was going to end up feeling like a finals match.

America seemed to be in the driver's seat as the women scored a goal off of Brazil right away. And their defense was on-point too, prohibiting the Brazilian team from even getting close to the American goal for the first twenty minutes of the game.

As halftime rolled around, the Americans had a 1–0 lead over Brazil, but Brazil's luck was about to change in a huge, controversial way that would still be talked about years later.

Australian referee Jacqui Melksham would insert herself into the game in a way she didn't intend.

As Brazilian forward Marta and American defender Rachel Buehler went head-to-head, Melksham called Buehler for a foul. Not only did she call a foul on Buehler for a play on Marta, she also handed her a red card, an immediate ejection from the game.

Things got even worse from there.

Just moments later, American player Hope Solo went against a Brazilian striker and was hit with a foul that resulted in a penalty kick for the Brazilian women. They were even given a second kick because the side judge on the field said that Solo moved forward before the PK.

Things were not going in America's favor and Brazil soon tied the game at 1–1.

The game was held in Dresden, Germany, with an even 50–50 split between fans rooting for Brazil and those rooting for America. But after the harsh calls by the refs, the crowd quickly turned on Brazil.[4]

As the game entered extra time, the questionable calls against the American women continued. In the 92nd minute of the game, Marta scored another goal against America, but it should have been moot because of a missed offside call by the refs. Therefore, Brazil now had a leg up over the US, a 2–1 lead that should have still been a tied 1–1 score.

America wasn't going down without a fight. By this point, they knew that the refs were dropping the ball, and they also felt the enthusiasm and support of the raucous German crowd that was cheering them on at every possible opportunity.

Stalling tactics by the Brazilian team meant that three minutes of extra time was added to the clock. It was during those three minutes that US star Megan Rapinoe took her chance and kicked the ball beautifully to her peer, Abby Wambach. Wambach made a good pass and headed the ball into the net.

The game was now tied again, 2–2 all sides.

The game would come down to penalty kicks and it was then that America was going to take advantage of their skills.

After the PKs were tied at 2–2, the third possible goal from Brazil was blocked by Solo. It was all coming down to American player Ali Krieger, who had actually played for the German league for the last four years.[5]

With all the pressure on her, Krieger knew that the fate of her team and the future of their time in the World Cup was all on her shoulders. And sure enough, she was ready for the call. She put the shot away with ease and the Americans officially beat the Brazilian team after a lot of spotty refereeing, bad calls, red cards that came out of nowhere, and fierce competition.

This historic match between the two teams is still talked about to this day for a number of reasons.

Firstly, the bad referee work is still looked at as a black mark on the team. There were many headlines after America achieved victory, and few of them were very positive and complimentary for the refs. Most of the stories said that the officials had done a poor job and had shown favoritism.

But the game is spoken of for reasons beyond that. The hard work of the American team is still celebrated, as it would be for many years to come. Over the years, the United States women's team made a name for themselves as a wholly dedicated, strong, talented group of women who never gave up fighting, no matter the odds. And even in a game when the officials were not doing their jobs correctly, the American players never lost faith or hope or belief in themselves.

Over the years, women athletes in soccer have done so much for the sport. More than the wins they have earned and the medals they now carry, they have also inspired so many young women, and have stood up for their rights when it comes to equality and fair pay for themselves and all female athletes.

It is disappointing and surprising to think that there was a time when female athletes weren't allowed to play in not only soccer, but any sport. Throughout the last 100 years, they have shown that they are capable of fighting just as hard as their male counterparts. And they have also shown that they will constantly instill hope in so many young people from every corner of the globe.

15

WHEN NEIGHBORS MEET IN THE WORLD CUP

I t's been more than 40 years, but the World Cup semifinal game from 1982 is still considered one of the greatest soccer matches of all time. Because of a nasty injury, bad referee decisions, and a penalty shootout that quite literally changed history, this game is still spoken of as one of the best ever.

The game was between West Germany and France. The game, held in the Ramón Sánchez Pizjuán Stadium in Seville, Spain, is still referred to as The Night of Seville by members of both countries.

Entering the game, tension and anticipation was high. Karl-Heinz Rummenigge, captain of the West Germany team, was ruled out before the match due to a hamstring injury. However, the loss of Rummenigge didn't mean that West Germany was out of the game or out of the running. Quite the opposite, in fact. They still had a great chance at winning the game.[1]

The game was intense from the opening minutes and the fans were eating it all up. Although the game was held in Spain, there were fans from both nations in attendance. The thousands of people were cheering on every kick of the ball and every single possession. In the 17th minute of the game the first goal was scored by the West German team, showing that they indeed did still have an advantage even though they were short-handed.

It was Pierre Littbarksi from West Germany who got things started with the kick. But France didn't wait long to score for themselves. Just ten minutes later, Bernd Forster of West Germany was caught holding a French player and that resulted in France being given a penalty kick. French player Michel Platini was able to turn that kick into a goal and the French team was officially on the board.

The game was off to a fairly normal and unspectacular start but things really started to heat up in the second half of the match. It was then that history was made.

Both sides really wanted to win and the passion and drive of the players became too hot as the second half of the game kicked off. That was obvious when West German goalkeeper Harold Schumacher threw his entire body into Patrick Battiston of the French team. This hit was devastating to Battiston, who lost consciousness and was left limp on the field. He was then carried off the field and the crowd went wild. The fans of the French team were beside themselves with rage against Schumacher, who wasn't sent off the field despite the intense hit to Battiston.

This is one of the many reasons why so many people remember this game so much. The fact that the refs weren't aware of—or just didn't care—how intense the injury was, is shocking. You would never see such a dull and calm reaction from game officials these days.

As for Battiston, he suffered a lot of damage. He lost three teeth and had cracked ribs and a damaged vertebra.

Following that rather nasty injury, the game went on and the intensity only grew.

The players had to play two 15-minute sessions of extra time since both teams had plenty of great opportunities in the remaining minutes, but the score remained 1–1 at the end of regulation.

An 11-yard shot from just beyond the box by French center-back Marius Tresor in the 92nd minute gave France their first-ever lead in the game, kicking off the first phase of extra time.

At this time, both of the teams were completely exhausted. Not only was it a tough match between two of the best squads in the world, but it was also a very hot day and all the players were feeling it.[2] In fact, multiple players were laid out on the field, hardly sure they could go on. Coaches on the sidelines were trying to inspire them, get them up and moving, and convince them to push harder and leave every last bit of themselves on the field.

Marius Tresor scored a goal for France and put them ahead for the first time in the game. Just moments later, it was none other than Rummenigge who came in to replace Hans-Peter Briegal in the match, despite the fact that he was still suffering from the nasty injury that didn't let him start the game.

There was a third goal from the French team during the 98th minute of this marathon game and gave the French men a 3–1 lead over West Germany. But Rummenigge for West Germany wasn't having any of it and he didn't intend to let his team let the opportunity slip away.

It was he who kicked the ball just six feet from France's goal, bringing the score to 3–2.

At this point, the French team was determined to do whatever was smartest to win the game and not give up their slim lead. So they stopped focusing on attacking as much as sticking to a strong defensive line. But that plan backfired as West Germany scored yet again three minutes into the second round of extra time.

The match was now tied and both teams were truly drained of any and all energy. It seemed like they wouldn't be able to go on and they were having trouble making their way up and down the field.

And that is where the most historic part of this game begins.

This 1982 game was the first-ever World Cup match to feature a penalty shootout. Today, we see shootouts all the time, even in World Cup Finals.[3] But even though both of the teams were beyond tired, they found enough energy to commit to the shootout.

Both teams scored a goal, taking the score to 4–4. But in the end, it would be West Germany who scored the winning goal, giving themselves a hard-fought, much-celebrated victory.

You've surely heard the saying "leaving it all out on the field" and the 1982 match between France and West Germany is the best example of that. Both teams were fighting hard, against each other, against the refs, against injuries, and against the elements.

16

THINGS HEAT UP IN THE SPANISH LEAGUE

"I'd say that Spanish football is probably the best I've ever seen."

— GARETH BALE

S o far, we have touched upon the fact that soccer is perhaps the most popular sport on Earth. True, it might not be wildly popular in the United States, even though it has made great gains over the last few decades, but it still reigns supreme in pretty much every other corner of the world.

That is especially true when you set your eyes to Europe, where soccer has been the biggest thing in the world for years now. Soccer is so popular in many parts of the world that life literally stops during certain games. Particular matches and competitions will see businesses, and truly entire cities, shutting down when the game is on.

Spain is perhaps one of the most devoted and diehard soccer nations in the world. For generations now, residents of that European country have been devoted to the game and have cheered loudly, proudly and wholeheartedly for their teams.

Two of the biggest teams in the country are Real Madrid and Barcelona. And since they are two of the biggest teams in a country that is so in love with soccer, you can bet that each time they face off against each other, people are going to pay attention. In fact, the entire country is glued to the screen when these two teams battle it out.

There are some people who feel that the massive popularity of both Real Madrid and Barcelona overshadow the fact that there are other clubs within the country that also play amazing soccer. But it's hard to not focus on these two teams when they play such amazing soccer, as they did during the wildly entertaining 2010–11 season.

El Clásico is one of the best soccer tournaments and it has accumulated millions of fans in its home country of Spain over the years. Even if you don't live in that country, it is always worth checking into if you're seeking a game to watch that is both fun and engaging, and played with expert skill.

El Clásico is the term used to refer to the matches that Real Madrid and Barcelona FC play against one another. Their athletes are of the highest caliber and these games always leave the fans satisfied.

Over the years, there have been some truly inspiring and jaw-dropping El Clásico games, including a few that are impossible to forget.

Let's go back to 2014 when Barcelona and Real Madrid were again at the height of their powers and were playing some stunning soccer. During the game, Messi scored a whopping three goals, two of which were penalty kicks, and he also gained an assist too. This was at the peak of his career and truly cemented him as one of the best soccer players not just of his generation, but also of all time.

Real Madrid tried to keep up and even the score but one of their best players, Ramos, was hit with a red card after about 60 minutes of play and this made their chances even smaller.[1] Messi, being the expert he was, took advantage of this and was able to bring home the gold for his team. In the end, the final score was Barcelona 4, Real Madrid 3.

But Real Madrid did score a good win in El Clásico in the 2013, when they were able to pull off a close but crucial 2–1 victory over their age-old rivals.

Perhaps one of the biggest games in El Clásico history would be the match in 2005, when players such as Beckham, Own, Ronaldo, Zidane, and Ronaldinho all came together to give fans a match they wouldn't soon forget. That game ended up being yet another win for Real Madrid, 4–2, but it's not the final score that people remember so fondly. Instead, it's the amount of star power that was on the field and the enormous amount of talent that was on display for every single second of the game.

Of particular note was the goal scored by Ronaldinho in the 73rd minute of the game. The way that the ball curved and seemingly found the goal made it seem as if Real Madrid's victory was written in the stars.

Finally, we must touch upon the wildly entertaining 2010 El Clásico game that was part of the Champions League. Two of the biggest rivals of the game, Barcelona's Jose Mourinho and Real Madrid's Sergio

Ramos, were set to go toe-to-toe and battle against one another.

Many people expected this to be a game that would be a nail-biter, closer than any that had come before, and full of anxiety and tension from beginning to end. But the most shocking thing about this match was the fact that it was actually a blowout loss for Real Madrid.

In fact, in the end the final score was Barcelona 5, Real Madrid 0. This was not the outcome that anyone really expected.

While it was a huge disappointment for fans of Real Madrid, this game stands out because it was such a strong display of the skill, talent and drive of Barcelona and it showed just how great they were. How could anyone not be impressed by that and their amazing victory?

Messi played in that game and another astonishing aspect of the 2010 game is the fact that he actually didn't even score a single goal. Sure, he had two assists, both of which were important, but to see the best soccer player alive not land a single goal was something that fans were shocked to see.

In the end, Villa scored two goals, Jeffen, Xavi, and Pedro each scored one themselves. As for Ramos, he was given a red card, which gave his opponents a huge advantage on the way to their win.[2]

Before this historic game started, many people thought that Real Madrid was going to be victorious. Mourinhio was in fact very confident in his team and publicly stated that the win was in the bag.[3]

Those who were rooting against him revealed the fact that not only did his team lose, but they lost in a total shutout.

This last game mentioned is one that will always be remembered because it shows that even the best teams can have their bad days. And when those bad days happen to be game days, it can lead to a startling, surprising and disappointing match that will leave fans on both sides of the game completely speechless.

Throughout history, few teams have inspired as many fans and drummed up as much emotion, both good and bad, as Real Madrid and Barcelona. Some of the biggest names in the game have played for these two teams and their histories are legendary.

Their rivalry is also legendary. That is why these El Clásico are so important to the history of the game and have been talked about so often. When you are looking to examine two teams who are almost always at the peak of their abilities and the top of their games, you should look no further than the star power and track records of these two squads.

When two of the biggest teams in soccer meet and battle against each other, it is always worth paying attention to. That is what makes the El Clásico event so exciting year after year.

17

RED CARD RECORDS

E ven if you don't know much about soccer, you surely know what yellow and red cards are. Both of these soccer staples have become such a big part of the game that they are now referred to in peoples' day-to-day lives. Have you ever heard someone warn a person that they are going to get hit with a "red card"? They might not even know what they are referring to but they still talk about it. That just goes to show how important and prominent the concept of yellow and red cards have become over the years.

But let's break down what a red or yellow card is and let's examine their history, where they came from, and what purpose they serve. Furthermore, let's talk about a few times throughout the history of soccer where players reacted strongly in a game and faced the consequence of receiving a yellow or red card.

We have discussed soccer ref Ken Aston before but we need to really dig into his mindset and his love of the game to figure out what drove him to create both yellow and red cards, quite literally changing soccer forever.

Aston actually was originally a school teacher before he entered the world of sports.[1] Being a teacher of young people taught him many things he needed to know about keeping people in line, making sure rules are followed, and trying to maintain order in the face of chaos.

All of this led to Aston deciding that it was time for him to try his hand at refereeing football, or soccer matches, years after teaching in school.[2]

Right away, Aston was met with the hard, intense, and sometimes violent world of soccer. And right away, he decided that things needed to change.

For one of his first high-profile jobs, Aston visited Chile in June 1962 to attend the World Cup. He was assigned to oversee a match in Santiago, the capital, where tensions were really high and it felt like there could be many fights, both in the stands of the arena and on the field between players. This contest was between Chile, the hosts, and Italy. Aston immediately saw that he was going to be faced with some huge challenges for the game.

Both teams were desperate to declare victory but things got so intense that many onlookers were astonished by the outcome of the game. The first foul of the game occurred after only 12 seconds and it was a brutal one. Shortly after that, Aston tried to dismiss Italian Giorgio Ferrini for kicking a Chilean player in the eighth minute.

However, it wasn't that simple back then because there simply wasn't a way to eject a player, even if they did something as heinous as kicking another player on purpose. The player couldn't be forced to leave because red and yellow cards had not yet been invented, and Aston did not understand Italian, which only made matters worse. In the end, Ferrini had to be pulled from the field by the player's teammates and stadium security as a result.

Aston did not dismiss Chilean player Leonel Sánchez for punching Mario David shortly before halftime. Aston requested that David leave the field after he kicked Sánchez in front of the referee a little while later because he was so furious. Once more, Aston lacked a method for requesting that the Italian leave the field and abandon the match.[3]

When the game was over and the melees were behind him, Aston was left with a feeling that something—anything—had to be done to change the future of the game and prevent another match like that one, which was called "the Battle of Santiago."

Aston had been faced with fully grown men, professional soccer players, who were acting worse than any of the school children he used to teach. And that is when he came up with the idea of yellow and red cards. Perhaps the elementary nature of the cards came from the fact that he had educated children for so many years. It was such a simple idea.[4]

By creating yellow and red cards, Aston figured that future referees would be able to handle the players on the field and eject them when necessary. More importantly, the colors were easy to understand and there would be no language barrier like Aston experienced during the Battle of Santiago.

It would be several years before yellow and red cards were adopted by the rest of the world and started appearing in games. In the 1970 World Cup in Mexico, cards were used and they were immediately a huge hit, loved by both fans and the refs on the field. They were easy to understand for players and for the people watching the game.

But just because they were now being used in soccer games didn't mean that players were going to change their ways. If a player received a yellow card, he or she was warned that they need to watch themselves because they could have derailed their team's chances. But a red card was an immediate ejection from the game, which was something that truly wasn't possible before Aston's idea.

Throughout the history of the game after the creation of yellow and red cards, there have been many instances of players getting wild, violent, and carried away—and the cards were there to keep them in line. Or try to, at least.

The 2006 World Cup game between Portugal and the Netherlands is today known as the Battle of Nuremberg because of just how intense and wild and crazy it became.

During that match, Russian ref Valentin Ivanov had to issue an enormous amount of cards. He had to hand out sixteen yellow cards and four reds as well. That is the highest amount of any FIFA tournament ever.

When the game was done, both sides only had nine men each playing. There were obviously four players who were kicked out of the game with their red cards and many more who received yellows.

The referee was well within his right to issue so many cards because the game was really filled with many nasty fouls, kicks, and multiple players lashing out at one another. But surprisingly, the referee's actions weren't defended by the president of FFIA, Sepp Blatter. He said that the referee was the one who deserved a yellow card for being too dramatic with the number of cards he issued.

Was that the worst of the worst? It probably was, but there have been many other events in recent memory where refs were forced to give out yellow and red cards like they were going out of style.

For example: Barcelona's visit to nearby rivals Espanyol in December 2003 set a new record for the most red cards in a Spanish Primera game. Now, you know that Spain takes its soccer games very, very seriously and the Primera games are the top of the top, the best there is. Therefore, you know that all eyes were on the game that garnered so many calls by refs.

In total, six men were eliminated, with two receiving straight reds and four being hit with double yellows. Amazingly, rather than a single large-scale altercation, each dismissal resulted from a different event. Many times throughout soccer history, multiple cards have been given out at one time because of a major fight between several players. But not during this match: this time each and every card was handed out because of multiple, distinct actions from players.

But if you're looking for more dramatic and shocking action on the field, don't worry, you're in luck. Because there have been many examples of the drastic events that have led to yellow and red cards since their invention. In fact, the rest of this book could consist of every time multiple yellows and reds were given out and you would be reading for hundreds of pages.

Let's take a look at another example of multiple yellow and red cards given out during one match.

In January 2009, things got so heated during one match that the referee's outrageous 19 red cards during a regional first-division match in Spain seemed downright comical by the end of the game.

But the violence that started between just a couple of players exploded in a huge way and was soon spreading throughout the teams like a wildfire. When Recreativo Linense received a red card from the ref, a massive riot broke out, and the match between Saladillo de Algeciras and Recreativo Linense was abandoned. There were now bigger concerns than which team was going to come out triumphant between the two. Now there were serious concerns about the well-being of the refs, coaches, and even the fans in the stands.

The referees tried to contain the chaos that was growing by sending nine more players from each side to the locker rooms. One after another, players were moving off-field, ejected so that the wild riot and violence wouldn't spread even more and become unstoppable.

It was lucky that no lives were lost during that game. The tensions were so high and tempers were flaring so much that fists and feet were flying left and right. In the end, the number of red cards handed out was astonishing, but it didn't really matter that much.

There is yet another game to highlight that shows the importance of yellow and red cards. That was when Argentine teams Claypole and Victoriano Arenas met in 2011 and set the record for the most red cards issued in a senior game.

And unlike the wild Spanish match from 2009, the violence during this game wouldn't only stay on the field. Sadly, it really did leap from the field to the fan-filled stands.

A huge brawl involving players, coaches, and spectators ensued in the second half, after two players were sent off in the first half following a flurry of risky plays and fearsome fights. And the people who were watching the game got in on the act too, fighting among themselves with anyone else they could get their hands on.

In a short amount of time, it felt like the entire game had turned into an all-out brawl that had the potential for a lot of damage and danger to anyone involved. But the refs only had the power to handle the people on the field. They would have to leave the fighting in the crowd to the local law enforcement authorities. Sure enough, the cops made short work of those causing chaos in the stands and arrests were made.

Back within the confines of the game, every player was given a red card by referee Damian Rubino, who also issued 14 further dismissals.[5]

There were 36 red cards in total.

As you can see, yellow and red cards came from a place of necessity. That is because some players and people associated with the game get too fired up about it and they can't seem to hold themselves back in the heat of the moment.

Because soccer is such a physical sport, and because there is such little protection on the bodies of the players, there can be serious injuries if athletes aren't kept in check, and if they don't follow the regulations of the game and keep their hands and feet to themselves. Soccer is a game that needs to be closely monitored because the risk of personal harm is higher than it is in many other sports.

That is why yellow and red cards are such a smart idea, created by a frustrated referee decades ago. It's both ironic and telling that someone who got his start teaching children was the one who created a game-changing idea that kept players, coaches, and fans in line for years and years to come.

18

THE FIRST ENGLISH TEAM TO
WIN A TREBLE

"It's not about the name on the back of the jersey, it's about the badge on the front."

— DAVID BECKHAM

There are few teams who inspire as much joy and opinion—both good and bad—as Manchester United.

Even the people who know hardly anything about soccer know that Manchester United, or Man U or Man United or just Manchester, as many people call them, is one of the biggest teams not only in Europe but the entire soccer world.

Sure enough, they have legions of fans all over the world and they are always spoken of when people talk about the best of the best in soccer. Partly because of the legends that have played for them (David Beckham, for example, played for Manchester) and partly because of all the success they have found.

Manchester United is now a team that is considered one of the very best and most legendary but there were times when they lacked some of the success that they have now. And there was a time when their chances in European championships actually weren't high. Did you know that Manchester U actually had a very long dry spell in which they had not won a European Cup since the 1960s? When 1999 rolled around, they were hoping to change all of that.

But it wouldn't be easy. It would, however, be downright historic.

There have been a lot of great games throughout the history of Manchester United but the game between them and Germany's Bayern Munich in May of 1999 is easily one of the very best, and showcases what makes this team so special and well-regarded throughout the world.

By the time the Champions League was coming, Manchester had already secured their Premier League title and FA Cup. Now all that was left was to fly over to Barcelona and face Bayern Munich, an age-old rival and truly one of the best soccer squads that was around at the time. Bayern had a lot on the line too. They were also attempting to secure their very own Treble after being named the top team in their home country of Germany.

As for Manchester, they hadn't won a European Cup since 1968, when most of the players now on their roster hadn't even been born yet![1]

The team was riding high, having just won their first Double in history and then repeating that feat again in 1996. So they had proven themselves, but they wanted to earn their Treble and they definitely wanted to beat Germany's best team.

This was a young squad that had a lot of skill, a lot of potential, and a lot of belief in themselves.[2] They would need all of that and more if they were going to take Bayern Munich.

Unfortunately, they also had some bad luck working against them at the time. Two of the team's biggest stars, Roy Keane and Paul Scholes, had been suspended. This meant that other players on the squad were having to change their roles, do new things, and pick up the slack. That is a lot easier said than done. For years, they had very specific spots on the field and tasks that were relegated only to them. Manchester had a very good thing going, a great rhythm, and an ability for all the players to read one another and play as a cohesive unit. But the change due to those suspensions put that all at risk.

It couldn't have come at a worse time. Bayern Munich knew that Manchester was adjusting to these changes, and they were hoping to take huge advantage of that in the Champions League game.

In fact, most people thought that Bayern had the game in the bag. They felt that the German team were the huge favorites and were going to easily put the short-handed Manchester United away.

The game got off to a quick and wild start in front of the surging mass of fans who were waiting to see if the German team could win or if Manchester would be able to fight back, impress, and prove the critics and naysayers wrong.

At first, it didn't look like they would.

Mario Basler's low free kick around the walls created by Manchester United gave the Germans a 1–0 lead after just six minutes, lifting Bayern up with a wonderful start. The crowd was on its feet and fans of Manchester United from all over the globe were already thinking that the worst-case scenario was going to come true and their team was going to fall, as predicted by so many.

Throughout the game, both teams created scoring opportunities, but Bayern particularly came close when Carsten Jancker's overhead kick at the conclusion of the second half hit the crossbar. It made it clear that Bayern obviously had an advantage in many ways and that the conventional wisdom might have been right. Maybe Bayerin Munich really was going to win that day.

Three minutes remained in the game, and it appeared that 1–0 might be the final score until Manchester United was given a corner. This was a big chance for Manchester United and its star, David Beckham. When goalkeeper Peter Schmeichel approached Bayern's penalty area, Beckham blasted a cross that narrowly missed the Dane.

Bayern wasn't fast enough after Beckham's kick. The inability to effectively clear the ball after a kick in front of the net by Manchester allowed Ryan Giggs to take a shot from the corner of the box. Although his attempt was poor, Teddy Sheringham, a substitute, calmly steered the ball over the line and past Bayern Munich goalkeeper Oliver Kahn to tie the score.

All over the world, the loyal followers of Manchester United saw an opening and an actual chance for their team to prove everyone wrong and actually win the game. But the match was only tied at the moment and that meant that much more needed to be done in order to secure victory.

It seemed like the game was going to enter extra time, but then Manchester United was given another corner kick. It was Beckham who was there again, ready to make his team proud. He sent the ball forward in a cross kick before it was headed toward the goal by Sheringham. It would be substitute Ole Gunner Solksjær who would be the fastest to react and stretch his foot out to land the ball in the goal.

Manchester United now had a 2–1 lead, which hadn't seemed possible just a few minutes before.

Sadly for Bayern Munich, time had run out and they didn't have a chance to bounce back or try to stage a comeback. The clock had been ticking for more than 90 minutes, and it seemed as if Manchester United had been smart to save all of their goals for the last few moments of the match. That meant that the game was coming to a close and Bayern Munich, despite so many people betting on them and thinking they'd be the victors, ended up being the loser of one of the biggest games of the year.[3]

Following the game, the team members were celebrated as heroes when they returned home. Obviously, much fanfare was made around Beckham, who had such a monumental and important performance. But Solskjaer was also cheered and heralded as one of the hottest, youngest, best new soccer players around.

That major victory against Bayern Munich was the start of a resurgence of Manchester United. It would mark the beginning of a huge stretch of years for the team, which would become better known all over the globe and would be called one of the best teams of their generation.

There would be many more wins ahead for Manchester United. But few would feel as good as the surprise, come-from-behind victory against Bayern Munich in the Champions League game. Despite what many people felt and what many analysts believed, they were able to rally together, take down their opponent, and score at the perfectly opportune time to claim a huge triumph.

19

WORLD CUP FREQUENT FLYERS

Did you know that Brazil is the only country to have participated in all 22 World Cup tournaments since the creation of the games? That's a stunning feat that is also a testament to just how much the nation respects and loves soccer and how great the talent from that country is.

But Italy isn't that far behind Brazil. In fact, they have been to 18 World Cups themselves, which is pretty close to the record set by Brazil.

This means that whenever the two teams come together, many people are going to be watching. Brazil and Italy are two titans of soccer and two monumental juggernauts in the World Cup. They are also both in the top five countries when it comes to the number of wins in the World Cup.

When speaking about Brazil and Italy and their history against one another in the World Cup, you have to speak about the 1970 game. But you also need to then talk about the 1982 rematch where everything changed.

The year was 1970 and as always, millions of people were tuning in to the World Cup to see who would come out on top. Throughout the tournament, both Brazil and Italy were neck and neck and considered the two best teams in the event. Therefore, it made total sense that they would be facing off against one another in the finale.

And it was then that Brazil made it all look so easy.

They handily beat Italy in the final World Cup match, 4–1, taking down Team Italia and becoming the champions of the world. That team was led by Tele Santana, who was instantly a hero for his country and one of the most popular soccer players in the world.[1]

It was a stinging defeat for Italy and it seemed like they might face the same fate again in 1982, because Brazil was entering the World Cup with a team just as strong as the one that led them to the championship in 1970.

Most everyone thought that Brazil was set to win the World Cup again.[2] But that didn't mean that millions of people weren't tuning in as the match between both sides started at Estadio Sarria in Barcelona on July 5, 1982.

This was the final second round group stage match for Group C in the Cup. The winner would go on to the next round and the loser would pack their bags and head back home. Brazil wanted to sail past Italy and make their way back to the final game and Italy was desperate to make sure they didn't suffer the same fate they did back in 1970.

Paolo Rossi got things started quickly, scoring the first goal with a head just five minutes into the match. Socrates for Italy made the team's comeback seven minutes later, tying the game. Then in the 25th minute, Rossi was back with another goal, proving that he was the team's most important player within the first half of the game.

68 minutes into the match, Falcao got hold of a pass from Junior and then shot the ball for Brazil. That evened the score at 2–2.

If the score stayed at 2–2, Brazil would have moved onto the next round because of the rules of the World Cup and how the points are awarded.

But it was Rossi—again—who provided the clutch move for Italy. In the 74th minute of the match, the ball made its way back to the Brazilian goal all because of bad footwork by the Brazilian team.[3] There simply wasn't enough time for Brazil to come back after that and the game was over with Italy, who were so horribly embarrassed just more than a decade before, coming out on top and moving on to the next round of the game.

In the end the impossible became possible as it was Italy who ended up the victors of the game, powered by the immense skill of Italian attacker Rossi's hat trick during the match. It was a stunning showing and performance from the team that so many people had written off and considered big underdogs.

The Brazilian team was strong—they scored two goals after all—but it wasn't enough to fight off and defeat the fired-up, rejuvenated, and driven Italian team. Much like many other people throughout the world and the soccer community, they didn't expect Italy to play as well or as hard as they did. They just didn't have a good enough defense to slow them down and stop them.

Since the 1970 and 1982 World Cups, both Brazil and Italy have remained institutions, not just in those games but in the soccer world as a whole. Few countries are as devoted to the game as these two and every win and loss is felt intensely by the loyal fan base that exists in both nations.

There have been many explosive, memorable games between these two countries but when people talk about the rivalry between Brazil and Italy, two of the best soccer countries on Earth, they often discuss the 1970 World Cup and then the 1982 game 12 years later when Italy was able to settle the score and get their ultimate revenge.

WHEN LIGHTNING STRIKES

There are few things in the natural world scarier than lightning. While watching a lightning storm in a safe environment can be amazing and even calming, the actual electricity and power of lightning is downright terrifying.

Did you know that lightning can heat the air around it to 50,000 degrees Fahrenheit? That means that anything lightning touches will be surely destroyed, burned or forever altered.

The good news is that the chance of being struck by lightning is very, very low. In fact, you have a better chance of winning tens of thousands of dollars in a scratch-off lottery ticket. Around 40 million lightning strikes hit the United States every single year but the chances of one of them striking you are just one in one million, with a 90 percent chance of survival. That is because the likelihood of lightning hitting you straight on and causing the sort of damage that would kill you is so rare that it's all but impossible.

However, there are certain parts of the world that are more susceptible to lightning strikes. Africa, for example, suffers a lot of lightning strikes every single year.[1]

In 1998, Congo in Africa was home to a horrible soccer incident that was caused by the violent power of Mother Nature. However, there is still a lot of debate around the accident and the lightning that caused it.

Two African teams, Bena Tshadi and Basangana were playing in the Kasai region of Congo, home to the Basangana team. The game was popular and there were dozens of people in the stands enjoying the match, which was tied at 1–1, when disaster struck.

Lightning came down from the sky in a split second. Immediately after the strike, multiple players collapsed to the ground as others around them weren't sure what had just happened. The commentators watching the game also weren't very sure what happened, although they both said they thought that lightning had hit the field.

Medics with stretchers and other team personnel rushed to the field, lifting the injured players off the ground and carrying them off.

The game was obviously stopped and didn't begin again. And the final results of the damage were traumatic and hard to believe. All 11 players for the Bena Tshadi team were dead because of the lightning strike and 30 fans in the crowd were also hurt.

The story is still talked about to this day as it was one of the biggest disasters in the history of soccer in Africa. But over the years, there have been a lot of myths and stories revolving around the lighting strike that took so many players down.

In the years since that incident, rumors of witchcraft and voodoo have led many to wonder some very serious and curious things about the lightning strike.

It is indeed interesting that the only reported deaths from the lightning strike during the match befell the traveling team who was visiting and trying to take down the local squad. Perhaps that is why some people started to think that otherworldly tricks were behind the lightning strike.

Witchcraft and voodoo are far more commonly accepted—and feared—in Africa. Unlike many other countries, there are people in communities there who truly believe that black magic can have an impact on the real world.

Additionally, there are many people who openly state they use black magic, voodoo, and witchcraft to influence the world around them.

If witchcraft really was the cause behind the horrible lightning strike that took 11 lives in 1998, it wouldn't have been the first time that people blamed magic for soccer incidents.

There is a witch doctor in Ghana named Bonsam, who has repeatedly said that he will do whatever it takes to make sure that his favorite soccer team comes out on top, including using witchcraft.[2]

Bonsam was rooting for his home team of Ghana as they were set to face off against the ever-popular, super successful Portugal soccer team in the 2014 World Cup. But shortly before the match was scheduled to begin, Portugal's biggest star, Ronaldo, said that he had been diagnosed with tendinosis.

The disorder causes stiffness and swelling throughout the body and obviously is something that can prevent soccer players from taking to the field. Most doctors believe that tendinosis is caused by micro-tears over a long period of time in the body.

But Bonsam said it wasn't micro-tears that caused the condition. He said it was him.

He told the local radio station:

> *"I know what Cristiano Ronaldo's injury is about, I'm working on him. I said it four months ago that I will work on Cristiano Ronaldo seriously and rule him out of the World Cup or at least prevent him from playing against Ghana and the best thing I can do is to keep him out through injury."*[3]

He went on to say that his witchcraft would only get progressively more powerful over time, eventually stopping Ronaldo from ever playing again: "This injury can never be cured by any medic, they can never see what is causing the injury because it is spiritual," he said. "Today, it is his knee, tomorrow it is his thigh, next day it is something else."

In reality, the medical condition was obviously caused by what doctors said: micro-tears in the fiber of the body that can eventually be recovered and repaired. Sure enough, they were and Ronaldo would go on to have a long and successful career, even though Bonsam said he had the power to stop him from ever kicking a ball again.

Even though black magic and witchcraft haven't really had an impact on the world of soccer, there are many people who look back at the horrible situation in Africa back in 1998 and believe that something dark and mysterious was behind the lightning strike that took down 11 players in the blink of an eye.

However, there is some debate about the 1998 lightning strike to this day. Because of the civil war that was ravaging Congo at the time, and the unreliability of local media, it's not entirely clear if all 11 people died or were simply injured. It is hard to get a straight story about the event, even all these years later.

But video footage of the event does exist, and it proves that lightning really did come down from the sky that day, ending the soccer match and injuring many.

There are many risks when playing soccer and many dangers exist on the field, even for the most advanced, professional, and careful players. But no game has ever been as dangerous as the one back in 1998 when lightning stopped the game and possibly took many lives.

21

THE GREATEST RIVALRY OF THE 20TH CENTURY

There are few things that can bring as much destruction, misery, and pain as war.

In fact, there is literally nothing else in the world that wages the damage that war can.

That is especially true when it comes to World War II, which is still the most horrible that was ever committed in human history. What made it so much worse was the fact that the war was truly a continuation of World War I, which came only a few decades before and struck through all of the world like a plague, especially in Europe.

It is estimated that between World War I and World War II, there were nearly 100 million deaths. That is more than nearly any other event in human history.

But the sheer startling amount of death was only one part of the pain that struck the world following these wars. After the wars, famine and disease and a serious depression set in in many corners of the world. In Europe, it felt like the darkness of the conflicts would never rise and the people of those nations would forever be bogged down by World War I and II.

But the 1966 World Cup was able to lift people up, put them back on the right path, and start to believe in happiness and hope again. And it remains one of the prime examples of the power of sports and the ability to change not only players but people all over the world.

The 1966 World Cup was the first one held in England since the end of the war in the 1940s. For a country that was still reeling from all they saw in the wars, this was a huge deal and carried the chance to give the country a great deal of hope after years and years of pain and dread.

It just so happened that England was set to face off against West Germany, a nation that was obviously a sore spot for England after years of them battling Germany in the wars. But those armed conflicts were seemingly behind both of these countries and fans from both nations were not rooting on their homelands because of the wars, they were cheering them on because they wanted their respective teams to win.

The match was held on July 30, 1966, during an amazingly bright and warm summer day. The blue skies wonderfully lit the vibrant green pitch as the game got off to a strong and startling start.

Right away, West Germany got off to a great start, scoring within 13 minutes of the start of the match[1]. But the enthusiasm from the crowd died down just a few moments later, when Geoff Hurst of England brought the ball into West Germany's net at 19 minutes into the competition.

It would be Hurst who would score two more times for his British team, after West Germany's Wolfgang Weber sank a shot at 90 minutes.

Hurst's second goal made good for England at 101 minutes into the match, as both teams were trying to secure a win in extra time. He would score again in the 120th minute but it was that second goal at minute 101 that would be talked about for a very, very long time and make the rivalry between both teams so much stronger and deeper.

The ball was kicked to Hurst from his teammate and he immediately directed it at West Germany's goal. The ball then hit the crossbar of the goal and then bounced down onto the goal line.

Hurst was triumphant, thinking he had just scored yet another goal for his determined team. He began to celebrate immediately. But there was confusion among other players for both teams. Did the ball go in or not? Did England just win the match?

Gottfried Dienst, the referee, wasn't quite sure where things stood so he turned to his assistant.[2] That assistant then determined that the goal was good and it gave England a huge advantage.

In the end, it would be England that won the game, ending the match with a 4-2 advantage. All of Wembley stadium was on its feet, cheering on the team and feeling the great weight of World War I and II disappear in seemingly seconds.

As for that questionable goal from Hurst, people have spoken about it ever since. In fact, there have been many studies and scientific experiments have proven that the ball might have actually not gone into the net fully. But it doesn't matter now because England won the game and with that victory they set a strong place for themselves in the history of soccer.

Although you would think that game would be the last to tie the wars to soccer matches, the truth is that there have been many instances of teams from former war rivals bringing up the past and talking about the wars.

For example, even in the 2002 World Cup, some English fans held signs that said "Stand up if you won the War" when playing against Germany. While some people might take these signs as a joking jest that could be playful, others find it offensive and sad that these terrible armed conflicts are still brought up decades later.

22

THE FATHERS OF SOCCER
BATTLING IT OUT

L iverpool. Arsenal. Easily two of the biggest teams to ever play soccer. To this day, they are rightfully known as the fathers of the game as it is now. These two teams have seen a lot, including a lot of success.

For the last few generations of soccer, both of these icons of the game have been towering giants when it comes to the skills and victories that other teams hope to somehow gain. But that doesn't mean they both haven't been through some rough times. Soccer is a game that has been around for decades upon decades now so even the best and most well-respected teams have experienced rough patches.

Both Liverpool and Arsenal are British teams and they were both there for their country when Britain needed them most. Because of a few horrific accidents, the 1980s were a very dark and troubling time for British soccer clubs and their fans. But Liverpool and Arsenal, through their hard work and dedication to the game and the fans who supported them, were able to turn a corner on that low period and were able to welcome in a new generation of great soccer.

In order to really understand just how Liverpool and Arsenal were able to help their country and the loyal fans of the game, you have to know what led up to that point and what had happened to the country.

The year was 1985 and Liverpool was set to face off against Juventus at Heysel Stadium in Belgium. Even though that was the national stadium for the country, it was in serious need of repair and was quite literally falling apart.[1]

In fact, the building was in such a bad state, and the cinder block material that constructed the outside of the stadium was so weak, that fans were able to simply kick holes in the walls and sneak into the stadium without buying a ticket.

That gives you a general idea of just how bad things were before the match, when thousands of people filed into the arena to watch Liverpool face off against Juventus.

Giampiero Boniperti, the president of Juventus, and Peter Robinson, the CEO of Liverpool, both appealed to UEFA pleading with them to choose a different location, like the Nou Camp in Barcelona or the Bernabéu in Madrid. UEFA turned down the chance to move the final to another location despite warnings and the reality that it would include two of the most popular teams in Europe.

The game could have welcomed many more fans and it could have made much more money for the powers that be but they still decided that the game would remain in Heysel. To this day, no one is really sure why a change wasn't made.

This all led to the horrible disaster that came during the game.

Around seven o'clock Belgian time, danger started to brew. A completely ineffective and flimsy chain-link fence divided Liverpool fans from Juventus supporters. Individuals from both camps were able to incite one another by hurling pebbles and rocks from the tumbling walls across the border.

The tossing of stones got harsher as kickoff drew closer. The Juventus area was where they were mostly being hurled from, which caused anger to grow among the Liverpool end spectators. Soon after, they made the decision to attempt to halt the stone-throwing, and they overwhelmed the police as they rushed through the space dividing the two groups of fans.

The Juventus supporters ran away from the incident and in the direction of a wall near the building's outside edge.

Because of the poor quality of the foundation, the structure could not withstand the power of a large number of fans and quickly fell.

Thirty-nine people lost their lives; however it wasn't because of the wall crumbling. Rather, as it collapsed, the pressure was released, and the victims died of suffocation. Over 600 fans also sustained injuries as a result of the event.

Football flags were placed over the bodies, which were spread out on the sideline of the field. Unluckily, a medical chopper arrived and tore off the blankets, making the bodies visible to everyone on the ground. When the Juventus fans at the other end of the stadium realized what had transpired, they started to riot. They tried to move toward the Liverpool end but were confronted by the police. They clashed, with some of the spectators throwing rocks, stones, and bottles at the Belgian officers.

In the aftermath of the tragedy, Liverpool fans were held solely responsible; however an inquiry into the incident forced several high-ranking officials, including a Belgian police captain, to admit fault as well.[2]

The government in England was compelled to respond. Prime Minister Margaret Thatcher advocated for the exclusion of English clubs from European tournaments.

After Heysel, English teams made an effort to be tighter about the types of persons who were permitted admission to their stadiums, including the establishment of a three-month suspension for troublemakers. Incredibly, Heysel was still used as a stadium for almost ten years.

The Liverpool Football Club didn't dedicate a memorial plaque to the tragedy's victims until 2010.

As bad as that accident was, another occurred during that decade that also left a dark stain on all of British soccer.

It was April 1989 and the new decade was just around the corner for soccer fans, who were excited for the 1990s and hopeful that the next ten years would be better than the last ten. But the 1980s would end in a terrible tragedy that shook all of the nation to its core.

At Sheffield Stadium, fans were eager to see their beloved Liverpool face off against Nottingham Forest in a semi-final. The atmosphere was described as "carnival-like" and boisterous, joyous. But a large crowd building up at the Leppings Lane turnstiles changed all of that in a matter of seconds.

There were so many people trying to pour into the stadium in that specific area that the conditions became very unsafe very quickly. As a way to alleviate the pressure of so many people, some of the authorities on hand attempted to open an exit gate. But it was too late and the intense crush of people pushing forward without any sort of guidance or control created what was called a "human cascade."

People fell, were trampled on, and more and more people fell on top of them. Things quickly got out of hand and it felt like a row of dominoes falling without any chance of getting back up.

In the end, 96 people lost their lives in the disaster.[3] The country was again shocked by the brutality and horrible sadness surrounding the event, and the fact that the death toll was actually larger than the stadium incident in Belgium years before was both startling and heartbreaking.

Later, a judicial inquiry was held to look into the tragedy. A final report concluded that the failure to close the tunnel was responsible for the nearly 100 deaths.[4] The report also pleaded with the British government to ban standing at football matches and move to an all-seater stadium system that wouldn't allow the sort of standing around and pressure from human bodies that led to the disaster.

These two accidents combined made it feel like things had never been so low for British soccer teams and fans. How could the game that was beloved by so many for decades be able to overcome the intense sadness of tragic events like these?

It would be both Liverpool and Arsenal who would lead the way and begin a new generation of soccer fandom.

In May 1989, these two teams were meeting in a Division One game, battling it out for the league championship. Liverpool was the odds-on favorite to win the match, which had the attention of the entire nation, a nation that was still reeling from the latest soccer tragedy.

In the previous eighteen years, Liverpool had won the league ten times and Arsenal hadn't scored a single win during that time. Plus, Arsenal hadn't won at Anfield, where the match would be held, in 15 years.

But just seven minutes into the second half, Arsenal was able to score the first goal. Then, with just a minute left on the clock, they scored yet another. This is a very important fact because Arsenal needed to win by at least two goals due to the difference in points in the tournament system.

Somehow, they were going to do just that.

Few people thought that Arsenal was going to win but when the final whistle blew, they stood tall and were able to conquer the team that everyone thought would win. It was an incredible feat and it was something that few people expected.

It also came at the end of a tough decade that featured not one but two horrible soccer tragedies that cost hundreds of lives, started governmental inquiries, and cast doubt on the future of the sport in the UK. It was a healing moment, a cathartic game that brought fans from both sides together. In fact, when the game was over, Liverpool fans stood and applauded the winning team, which officially put an end to the ugliness that had preceded that game.[5]

Over the next few years, soccer experienced a huge rebound in England and remains the biggest sport in that country. The 1980s were not easy for soccer teams and fans but the resilience of those who support the sport kept it alive and led to one of the most memorable games of all time.

The two tragedies that struck the soccer world in the 1980s are still talked about to this day and the incidents have led to many positive changes with regard to the safety of fans. But perhaps the most lasting impact of these incidents is the remarkable fact that fans of the game were able to come together and heal the wounds that were still fresh.

They didn't do this as simply soccer fans or fellow countryfolk. They did it as people who were helping other hurt people and using the sport they all loved to mend broken hearts.

23

PELÉ'S LAST GAME

Just like with any sport, the people who love soccer have certain athletes and icons of the game that they hold above everyone and everything else. It is only natural that there will be some heroes of the game who will be more well-regarded than others and will go down in history as some of the best of all time.

You have to be a very exceptional soccer player to be considered among the best. But how good do you need to be to not only be considered among the best but quite possibly the *very* best? How does someone rise above the rest of the top tier of the game and be considered the greatest to ever play the game?

It's not often that any sport has a general consensus about who the greatest of all time is. Basketball players debate if Michael Jordan, Kareem Abdul-Jabbar, or LeBron James rule their sport, for example. But when it comes to soccer, most everyone can agree that Pelé is clearly the frontrunner for the best soccer star to ever grace the field.

For years, Pelé gave his heart and his soul—and his body—to the game that he loved so much. The game, and its billions of fans, loved him back. They cheered him on, supported him, and pulled for him through thick and thin, and the ups and downs that come with any professional sports career.

What is it that made Pelé the greatest? How did he rise above the rest and claim such a huge spot in the history of the game?

When you look at his career—and especially his final game—you can see the sort of player, and man, this once-in-a-generation player really was.

What is it that constitutes greatness? And, more importantly, what is it that constitutes the greatest of all time? If we are going to consider Pelé the best soccer player to ever touch a ball, we have to know how he is being judged.

You really need to look at the amount of victory that someone achieves in their lives and that is usually measured by the amount of trophies that a player earns.

When you look at all the achievements and victories Pelé had during his life, you will see that he was the youngest winner of a World Cup and the youngest scorer in the game, at the tender age of just 17 years old.

He was the top scorer of his Brazilian National Football Team and had the most assists in the World Cup.

Throughout his life, he scored nearly 1,000 goals during his 1,363 games.[1] That would be enough to make him one of the best of his time but when you add that to the other list of achievements during his career, Pelé is clearly ahead of the rest.

When it comes to soccer, the World Cup is the gold standard of greatness. If a soccer player is able to make it that far, they are surely one of the best in the world. The fact that Pelé made it to the World Cup numerous times *and* set records there shows that he was one of a kind.

But you also have to look at how long he played the game and the impact he had on the other players that came up after him. Pelé is still considered a god by nearly all soccer players. No matter their age or the style that they play, they look to Pelé as the one they aspire to be like. They think of the way he led his teams, the goals he scored, and the way that he devoted himself to the game.

He started the game at a young age and after that point he never looked back, pouring himself into the sport. Unlike nearly any other athlete in similar sports, Pelé's prime lasted for nearly 15 years.[2] You can't find many other athletes who are able to outshine everyone else on the field for so long. Soccer is a very physical sport, it can be very draining and age will only make that worse. But age didn't seem to have an effect on Pelé, who remained at the top of his game from his first game onward.

The thing that is so amazing about his longevity is that the game around him changed drastically during that time. Everything, from the type of players in the game to the type of field they ran on, became very different during Pelé's career. Yet he was still the top of the top despite all the evolution and changes to soccer.[3]

Imagine falling in love with a sport at a young age and then watching it change and become so much harder and more competitive. And then imagine remaining the very best at that sport. That's what Pelé did, and that's one of the reasons why he's considered the greatest of all time.

To this day, champion soccer players attempt to emulate Pelé and play the sort of game that he perfected during his career. It's been nearly 50 years since Pelé was at the top of his game but people are still trying to play like him.

Lastly, you have to judge Pelé's career by the impact he had. Not only did he outplay everyone and teach millions of young boys and girls how they should master the game, but he also spread awareness about soccer all over the globe. While soccer had been very popular in many corners of the globe before Pelé picked up a ball, he made it even more popular.

From his home country of Brazil, to nations more reluctant to embrace soccer like the United States, Pelé became a household name all over the world. He was simply known as *the* face of soccer for his entire career. He brought soccer into the homes of millions and showed them the value of the game.

All these years later, Pelé is still looked at as a man who changed the game—and a man who remained the best at it from the start to the end of his career. His impact on other soccer players and the game as a whole are immeasurable and simply cannot be overstated.

One of the best things about Pelé's career is that it ended in such a celebratory, special, unique way. In fact,

Pelé's final game is still spoken of to this day as an example of pure class and championship love for the game and the people who celebrated him for years.

Pelé hung up his jersey on October 1, 1977, after nearly 20 years of playing professional soccer. The final game was in New Jersey on a dark, dreary and rainy day. Yet, thousands of people showed up to wish the greatest soccer player of all time well.[4]

For his final game, Pelé played for the two professional teams that had signed him, the New York Cosmos and Santos of Brazil. For the first half of the match, he suited up for the Cosmos and for the second half of the game, he played for Santos.

He tied the game at 1–1 near the conclusion of the first half, with a stunning goal for the Cosmos on a free kick from about 30 yards out to cap an illustrious career. Ramon Mifflin, who replaced Pelé when Santos joined them for the second half, scored the game-winning goal for New York, giving them a 2–1 victory.

The game was an exciting one and the fans were cheering, chanting, and crying tears of both joy and sadness from the kickoff until the very end. But in many ways, the game was secondary to the celebration that was commencing. It was a great celebration of Pelé's career and all he had done for the game.

Before the game got started, nine groups of children came forward onto the field to present Pelé with flowers. The suffering and well-being of children all over the world was always of great importance to Pelé, who spoke directly to the crowd about it:

> *"I want to take this opportunity to ask you, in this moment when the world looks to me, to please take more attention to the young ones, to the kids all over the world. We need them too much. I want to ask you because I believe that love is the most important thing we can take from life, because everything else passes to say with me three times: love! Love! Love!"*

But the heartfelt sentiment didn't end there. During halftime of the game, Pelé gave his Cosmos jersey to his father Dondinho, who had supported him since the very beginning.[5] Pelé's dad was a soccer star himself and he understood that his son had surpassed anything he had ever done. The tears in his eyes said it all.

There was one another person who earned a jersey on that historic day. Pelé gave his number 10 Santos jersey to Waldermar de Brito, who was the man who found Pelé at the young age of 12 and helped him grow, achieve success, and become the star that he was. Without the support of the two men who were carrying his jerseys, Pelé would have never been able to reach the heights he did and change the game forever.

The crowd, featuring hundreds of reporters and photographers and celebrities, waved and cheered and chanted Pelé's name as the exhibition game came to an end on that rainy afternoon.[6] After the match concluded, Pelé was done playing soccer professionally, heading directly into the history books where he rightfully belonged.

Years have gone by since that day, and Pelé has now passed away, and yet he is still talked about as the best of the best, the man who changed soccer. Not only was he the best to ever touch the soccer ball and take to the field, but he revolutionized the game and the way that people look at it.

THE WEATHER HAS THE LAST SAY

As mentioned multiple times before, soccer is a sport that can quite literally bring people together. True, it can tear people apart if fans and players don't mind their tempers, but soccer is one of the few events that can really mend the relations of people, countries, and the entire world.

But soccer is also an outdoor sport, which means it sometimes has to battle with the elements and the will of Mother Nature. What happens when good intentions are met by the whims of nature? Well, it can lead to a bizarre, unique, downright comical soccer match that was made with the best of intentions but went horribly—and hilariously—off track.

The year was 1945 and Europe was still reeling from World War II and attempting to put that massive event behind it. Two of the countries that had fought in the war, Germany and England, were still at odds politically and the future looked bleak when it came to their relations.

Leave it to soccer to step in and try to fix things.

At the time, the Dynamo Moscow team was the greatest team out of the USSR. When it came to Russian sports, they were head and shoulders above the rest and people in other parts of the world were aware of their power.

The English Football Association thought it would be a great idea to invite the Dynamo team to the UK to play against some British teams. They saw this as a good way to build friendships between the sports leagues in both countries, even though the political figures running those nations were still at odds.

The USSR team thought this was a good opportunity to raise their profile and perhaps beat a few teams who were considered the greatest in the world. Certain British teams were called the best on Earth and Dynamo Moscow wanted to take a shot at bringing them down, at least in exhibition games.

Their trip to the UK didn't get off to a great start because of certain language and cultural barriers, but soon Dynamo was suiting up to play against British soccer teams.[1]

Dynamo's first game against Chelsea was exciting but it ended in a 3–3 tie. This was a good start, but it paled in comparison to the next game, against Wales. During that match, Dynamo Moscow showed why they were the cream of the crop in Russia.

They beat Wales easily with a huge 10–1 victory. The local newspapers reported on the big win and it seemed like Dynamo were well on their way to taking a few British teams down a couple of notches, and also raising their own profile internationally.

Then came the third game, when both teams wouldn't have to just compete against each other but also the wills and wants of fickle British weather.

The Dynamo Moscow team was facing off against Arsenal, who were unquestionably one of the strongest teams on Earth. This was Dynamo's biggest target, the team that they wanted to beat more than anyone else. Dynamo didn't want to take any risks, they wanted to win, and they wanted to win big.[2]

Right off the bat, the Russian team scored with a big goal 33 seconds into the friendly match. However, Arsenal caught up and held a 3–2 lead at halftime. But then the fog started to roll in and things got very bizarre.

Britain is known for its thick, heavy, unstoppable fog. And the match between Dynamo Moscow and Arsenal found that out the hard way. When the fog settled on the field, it made it nearly impossible to see just a few steps ahead.

This caused utter chaos. For at least 20 minutes, Dynamo Moscow actually had 12 people on the field at one time, breaking regulations. But there was no way for the referees to notice because they could hardly even see the whistles in their hands.

The visibility got so bad that one Arsenal player was sent off the field after a foul but then he came back on and continued to play, completely unnoticed.

Because of the fog and the invisibility it provided, players tackled each other, committed hard fouls, and played as if they weren't being watched by the refs. In the end, the Russian team was able to pull out a 4–3 victory, although there is some debate if the score was actually much higher or much lower. It was very hard to even see the ball for most of the game.

In the end, this match didn't do much to help international relations between the two teams. If anything, it made both sides dislike each other more. But it was an example of two things: the importance of soccer and its power to bring people of all types together—and the nasty and unpredictable nature of British weather.

WHEN RETURNING HOME DEPENDS ON THE GAME

B ecause soccer is played in every part of the world, that means that it is popular in countries that are going through some serious—often scary—changes. And while soccer can rise above all of that and change people and nations for the better, sometimes the people who love and play the game have to compete with the politics and government of their homeland.

That is what happened during the 1974 World Cup to the nation of Zaire.

Today, Zaire is known as the Democratic Republic of the Congo. It is one of the biggest and most well-known nations in Africa and during this point in the 1970s, it was going through some major changes. A coup had resulted in Colonel Mobutu Sese Seko taking over power of the country.

Mobutu was not a good man, not by a long shot. In fact, when he rose to power, one of the first things he did was commit political executions of his enemies and funnel power into his own interests rather than the interests of the compatriots he said he would serve.

One of Mobutu's major focuses was bringing major soccer success to his country. He put a lot of money into the country's national team and was intent on making them succeed and reach the World Cup.

He wanted to put Zaire on the radar of many other countries, showing their ability, skill, determination, and power. He thought that soccer could be the key to doing so.

After beating Cameroon, Ghana and Morocco, Zaire actually finally qualified as the first sub-Saharan country to reach the World Cup.[1] As a way to celebrate, the country's leader Mobutu lavished his team with fancy gifts and the promise of fame and fortune if they continued to win. He promised them all huge bonuses if they made Zaire proud at the World Cup.

However, the truth was that Zaire, while filled with some talented players, was still an underdog team as they entered the World Cup. The World Cup consists of the best teams in the entire world and Zaire just couldn't hold a candle to them. They weren't going to be able to get far despite what Mobutu wanted.

Sure enough, the team lost their first game 2–0 against Scotland. And Mobutu was incredibly upset and made his opinion widely known. He immediately withheld the cash bonuses that had been promised.

This reaction from their leader earned the anger of the team that was trying to perform well on the world stage. Therefore, the team's captain said that the national team wouldn't play in the second game.

But their dictator at home wasn't having any of that and demanded that they continue to play. He threatened even more damage to the team, in multiple ways.[2]

They were good to their word and definitely showed up for the next game, which just so happened to be against world champions Brazil. There was almost no way for them to score victory against the best team on Earth. They knew this, but they also knew they promised to play. So they played, in a way.

For the entire game, the team from Zaire resorted to time-wasting tactics. They obviously weren't trying to win and they even hesitated to touch the ball at times. Brazil wasn't quite sure what to do with all of this, although they started to rack up a win. Soon enough, they had a 9–0 lead on Zaire but the team didn't care at all.[3]

It was a bizarre moment, one unlike any other that had happened in the World Cup before. Zaire got trounced but they weren't even trying. They were protesting the treatment they received from their country's leader and they made it clear to anyone watching that they weren't trying.

The team from Zaire definitely did have talent that year and they deserved their spot in the World Cup. The fact that their achievements were overshadowed by their corrupt leader is very unfortunate. Was it smart to resort to time-wasting tactics? Maybe, maybe not. But you can't blame them for the anger they felt.

CONCLUSION

British soccer player Gary Lineker once said that soccer is basically a game of 22 men chasing a ball for 90 minutes.

Sure, that is a good way to describe the basics of the game, but after reading these varying stories gathered throughout the history of the game, you have seen that soccer is so much more than that. It's more than just a ball and a net, it's more than just 22 people running around the field.

Soccer is a lot more than that.

Soccer is steeped in deep history that reflects countries from all over the world. Many soccer games are mirror images of the world they are played in. They touch upon the strife of people and nations, they also dig into international relations, and major world events, too.

If you want to look into the cultures of the world and examine their people, you need to look at soccer. It is so much more than just a game. It is a way for people to come together and to join with one another or push against each other via the game.

Looking back at the stories we have just experienced, you have seen that soccer has held some great heroes and great moments too. From Ken Aston, the school teacher who became a ref, then made the yellow and red cards, to Pelé and the ways that he changed soccer, there are titans of the game who elevated the game even higher.

There have been moments that have brought fans together, like the numerous World Cup victories of Brazil and Italy to the tragic accidents in England in the 1980s. There have been moments that have seemed larger than life and hard to believe, like when lightning struck the field during the middle of a game or when a soccer game actually led to war between two countries.

From David Beckham to the Uruguay soccer team to the women players who helped propel the game forward, soccer is full of notable characters and very notable moments.

When you think about soccer, you should think about all the stories we have gone over and you should think about the effects of the game on millions, if not billions, of people. Think of how they joined together to celebrate Liverpool after a pair of brutal accidents in the 1980s cast doubt on the future of the game. Think of how they cheer on and chant for those injured on the field in numerous ways. Think of how they all stood in respect for Pelé during his last game.

That is what soccer is about. It's about people coming together and becoming more than just strangers cheering on a game. There is something about soccer that shows the humanity of the world.

Now that you have learned so much about the game, the teams that play it, and their rivalries and histories, the upcoming Champions League will be even more interesting. Now that you know so much more about soccer, you can enjoy and respect it even more deeply. Consider yourself a soccer fan.

Before you close this book and continue your love affair with soccer, leave a review to reflect the impact this book had on you and your knowledge of all things soccer. As the years go on, future generations need to learn more about the game and the people who have turned it into the global institution it is. Many people have devoted their lives to soccer in order to make it as big as it is now. As a sign of respect, we need to keep telling their stories. Any review you leave will help us keep their stories, their histories and their memories alive.

Soccer is for everyone. It is a game that can touch the hearts of people all over the globe. It is truly the peoples' game. And now it is *your* game too.

REVIEW QR CODE

If you have enjoyed these tales and maybe even learned something, let me know. If the book has fulfilled its promise, please put up a review and spread the word to those who will enjoy it. I hope it will be possible to bring more stories to readers.

Review QR Code

Review link

review/ref=cm_cr_othr_d_wr_but_top?
ie=UTF8&channel=glance-
detail&asin=B0BTTFW3MZ

mail: lingsterbooks@gmail.com

instagram: @roy_lingster

Facebook: Roy Lingster

NOTES

1. THE GAME THAT LED TO A 100-HOUR WAR

1. The United Fruit Company actually owned 10% of the land, which made it very hard for an average farmer to buy the land because they couldn't compete with such a big company.
2. At the time, the population of El Salvador, 3.7 million, was 40% larger than that of Honduras.
3. Following this game, eighteen-year-old Amelia Bolanos committed suicide, allegedly because of the loss of El Salvador. Newspaper El Nacional would later say, "The young girl could not bear to see her fatherland brought to its knees."
4. 1,700 Mexican police were on hand because of the chance of violence.

2. FRESH WOUNDS OF A DIFFERENT KIND

1. Already a hero in his homeland, Maradona would later be the first player to set the world record transfer fee twice, once in 1981 and again in 1984 for both 5 million pounds and 6.9 million pounds.
2. The Falklands War took place from April 1 to June 14, 1982, a total of just two months and twelve days.

3. HOW MANY PENALTIES?

1. Penalty kicks are also given to players who are fouled in the penalty area of the field, which is the large, rectangular area

around the goal at both ends of the field.

2. Juventud Alianza was originally formed in 1905 under the name Atletico Juventud

3. Founded in 1914, General Paz Juniors is one of the oldest soccer teams in the country

4. THE GREATEST SOCCER COMEBACK

1. A soccer game is typically about 90 minutes long.
2. That is an average of six goals between both teams for the entirety of the season. Those are high numbers for most soccer games.

5. WHEN ONE'S OWN GOAL ISN'T ENOUGH

1. There are 11 positions in each and every soccer game.
2. The referee was actually working his last game so he wanted to keep the ball for himself as a piece of memorabilia.
3. Nicholl would later go on to play for multiple more teams and actually become a team manager. Throughout his career he won 51 Northern Ireland full international caps.

6. IT'S NOT OVER TILL THE WHISTLE BLOWS

1. The most famous of these murders would be the death of Otavio Jordo da Silva Cantanhede, a 20-year-old Brazilian amateur football referee, who was stabbed to death during a game he refereed in June 2013 and was then lynched, beheaded, and quartered by onlookers.
2. These were two of the most famous Danish teams of the time.
3. While a yellow card doesn't always call for expulsion, a red card leads to an immediate ejection from the field.

7. THE STRANGEST TRANSFER
PAYMENTS EVER

1. Neymar was moving from Paris Saint-Germain from Barcelona.
2. That comes out to over 500 kg of pork!
3. Converted to the metric system, that would be about 165 pound of shrimp for the player.

8. GOALS GALORE!

1. This was just before the 2024 World Cup, in which many people were protesting the human rights abuse charges that had been leveled at the host nation of Qatar.
2. It was a round-robin tournament, in which each team would play each other twice, in a series of 12 games over the course of 11 days.
3. Due to the on-field protest, Adema players ended up touching the ball only one time throughout the entire game.

9. HAT TRICKS AREN'T ENOUGH FOR
RONALDO

1. Real Madrid would secure a 9-1 victory, which was the biggest defeat of La Liga since 1967.
2. This broke Real Madrid's record by scoring 230 goals in only 203 matches.
3. In his 2007 season, Ronaldo put up an amazing 42 goals for the year.

10. URUGUAY RISES TO CONQUER THE WORLD CUP

1. The modern World Cup has 32 participants.
2. Brazil's Deputy Sports Minister publicly said, "In this country you are either first or you are last," which shows just how seriously the country was taking the game.
3. There were sadly two reports of suicides committed in Brazil because of the loss of the World Cup.

11. THE BATTLE OF SANTIAGO

1. An Argentian journalist who was mistaken for one of the Italian writers was beaten by Chilean residents.
2. Both journalists had actually fled the country for their own safety.
3. It would be Czechoslovakia who won the World Cup that year.
4. He would later be appointed to the FIFA Referees' Committee and served on it for 8 years. He would later go on to create the concept of the yellow and red cards.

12. SOCCER'S WORST INJURY

1. The West Ham manager, Alan Curbishley, was upset about the foul against Dyer, saying, "I think the Bristol Rovers player has got to be very disappointed with his tackle."
2. Totti's injury was so nasty that surgery was required on him that very evening.
3. Believe it or not, Lienen would be practicing with his team again in just 17 days!

14. WOMEN SETTING THE STANDARDS IN SOCCER

1. The St. Helen's Ladies easily won that game, 4-0.
2. At the time, they said that women playing the game was unsuitable for the gender, which was an excuse that many institutions relied on when they were banning women from participating in things.
3. The two teams had met in the last World Cup just four years before. Both teams shared the same hotel and when Brazil beat the US, it was said that they rubbed it in their opponents' faces. The bad blood remained years later during this match.
4. Following the red card and the foul, Marta from Brazil was booed every single time she even touched the ball.
5. This fact made her all the more favorable to the Dresden crowd.

15. WHEN NEIGHBORS MEET IN THE WORLD CUP

1. In fact, most analysts of the time thought that West Germany had the advantage over France, despite the loss of the team captain.
2. It was 37 degrees during the match, which converts to about 98 degrees Fahrenheit.
3. The 2022 World Cup was determined by a PK shootout, for example.

16. THINGS HEAT UP IN THE SPANISH LEAGUE

1. The team was now forced to play the rest of the match with just 10 players.
2. He received the red card for not being able to control his emotions and hitting an opponent. When he walked off the field, the

response from fans both for and against Ramos was intense and loud.

3. He had just had seven impressive league victories, giving him every reason to believe that he and his team would walk away with the big win.

17. RED CARD RECORDS

1. Aston was also a soldier during World War II before he started his career as a teacher in 1953.
2. He started this second career in 1962.
3. Commentator David Coleman later described the match as "The most stupid, appalling, disgusting and disgraceful display of football, possibly in the history of the game."
4. Aston said he got the idea for the yellow and red cards when he was stopped at a traffic light on the way home from the match.
5. It wasn't just players who received red cards and were kicked out of the game. Coaches as well as substitute players were also ejected.

18. THE FIRST ENGLISH TEAM TO WIN A TREBLE

1. At the time, they had only reached the semi-finals for the Champions League.
2. Some of the biggest stars on the team at the time included Gary Neille, Ryan Giggs, Nicky Butt, and a young man named David Beckham.
3. Referee Pierligui Collina would later say of the match: "I will always remember it for different reasons: first of all, the reaction of the Manchester United supporters when they scored the second goal – it was an incredible noise, like a lion's roar."

19. WORLD CUP FREQUENT FLYERS

1. He would later become a very successful football manager, remaining popular throughout his life until his death in 2006.
2. 50% of the best sports analysts for the World Cup said that Brazil would win it all.
3. One more goal would be scored, one from Giancarlo Antognoni in the 86th minute of the game. It would have been the fourth for Italy but it was incorrectly disallowed because of an offside call by the refs.

20. WHEN LIGHTNING STRIKES

1. Kabare in the Democratic Republic of Congo experiences about 205 lightning strikes a year while Kampene gets hit 176 times.
2. "Bonsam" translates to "Devil".
3. The witch doctor claimed that he was able to create a special spirit that infected Ronaldo by killing four dogs.

21. THE GREATEST RIVALRY OF THE 20TH CENTURY

1. It was Helmut Haller who was the first to score for West Germany, bringing great cheers from the German fans who had traveled thousands of miles to witness the anticipated match
2. The assistant, Tofiq Bahramov, knew at the time that the decision was about to make could define his career and his life.

22. THE FATHERS OF SOCCER
BATTLING IT OUT

1. The stadium was over 50 years old at the time and there was evidence of it collapsing in certain parts.
2. Additionally, fourteen Liverpool fans were convicted of manslaughter.
3. The youngest victim was 10 and the oldest was a 67-year-old fan.
4. This decision was called "a blunder of the first magnitude."
5. This game would later inspire the feature-length film '89 as well as the book Fever Pitch by Nick Hornby.

23. PELÉ'S LAST GAME

1. 1,279 to be exact.
2. Although some people argue that it was longer—or shorter—most can agree that he was in his prime between the years 1958–1970.
3. For example, yellow and red cards were created during Pele's career, something that he was able to quickly adapt to.
4. The actual official number of people at Giants Stadium that day is 75,646.
5. Pele's number 10 is still worn by many soccer fans all over the world.
6. In the crowd were 340 reporters and celebrities such as Muhammad Ali.

24. THE WEATHER HAS THE LAST SAY

1. When the team arrived with a translator and radio commentator, the commentator was critical of the welcome they received. They didn't like that there weren't flags, music, or flowers upon the arrival of the Russian team.
2. In fact, the Russian team demanded a Russian referee for the game, as a way to even the odds and make the game more fair.

25. WHEN RETURNING HOME
DEPENDS ON THE GAME

1. Morocco actually boycotted the game, which still counted as a victory for Zaire and helped get them closer to the World Cup.
2. Although there is no definitive proof, reports say that Mobutu threatened the lives of the team if they didn't show up to the next game.
3. The refs had to get involved, threatening to give Zaire yellow or red cards if they didn't actually attempt to play in the game.

Made in the USA
Middletown, DE
17 December 2023

45845377R00123